RIDE
WESTERN
STYLE

RIDE WESTERN STYLE

A GUIDE FOR YOUNG RIDERS

Tommie Kirksmith

HOWELL BOOK HOUSE

New York

MAXWELL MACMILLAN CANADA

Toronto

MAXWELL MACMILLAN INTERNATIONAL

New York   Oxford   Singapore   Sydney

All photographs are by Gene Brown's Photos, Gainesville, Texas, unless otherwise credited.

Howell Book House
Macmillan Publishing Company
866 Third Avenue
New York, NY 10022

Maxwell Macmillan Canada, Inc.
1200 Eglinton Avenue East, Suite 200
Don Mills, Ontario M3C 3N1

Macmillan Publishing Company is part of the
Maxwell Communication Group of Companies.

Library of Congress Cataloging-in-Publication Data

Kirksmith, Tommie.
Ride western style : a guide for young riders / Tommie Kirksmith.
p. cm.
Includes index.
Summary: Presents basic instructions for riding stock seat or
Western style.
ISBN 0-87605-895-0
1. Western riding—Juvenile literature. [1. Western riding.
2. Horsemanship.] I. Title.
SF309.3.K57 1991
798.2'3—dc20 91-18579
CIP
AC

This book is not intended as a substitute for professional advice and guidance in the field of horseback riding. A young person should take part in the activities discussed in this book only under the supervision of a knowledgeable adult.

Macmillan books are available at special discounts for bulk purchases for sales promotions, premiums, fund-raising, or educational use. For details, contact:

Special Sales Director
Macmillan Publishing Company
866 Third Avenue
New York, NY 10022

10 9 8 7 6 5 4 3 2 1

Printed in the United States of America

CONTENTS

ACKNOWLEDGMENTS

———◆◄●►◆———

The person primarily responsible for this book is my editor, Madelyn Larsen. She suggested that I write it.

Gene Brown took time from his busy studio to take all but two of the photos and prepare them for publication.

David Hart, a local artist, improved my illustrations.

Deb Bennett, Ph.D., clarified what I'd always felt was so—namely, that boys and girls are built differently as riders. I've been a "Dr. Deb" fan ever since she began writing for *Equus* magazine. She has a profound gift for explaining a horse's structure in terms that make sense.

Bruce H. Blake, president of Lexington Safety Products, Inc., donated the Western Safety Helmet pictured in Chapter 1. This new product will appear throughout my next book, on Western performance.

Gene took some photos at Shirley Robben's place nearby, using Sunny Gayden and her AQHA barrel racer, Rooster-ama.

Most of the pictures, however, were taken locally at the Jones Ranch, owned by Reagan and Jones Vestal. Their grandchildren, Cyrus and Erin Vestal, were perfect models.

When Reagan bought a pair of three-year-old colts from Jack Brainard, I worried that Cyrus and Erin would get hurt. I stopped worrying after I met the horses and watched the youngsters ride them. Both geldings are living proof of the success and dependability of Jack Brainard's training program. But seasoned cow pony Bo is Cyrus's favorite horse and the one he rides in these pictures. Erin and Cyrus are not interested in competing. They'd rather ride for fun and help their dad and granddad work cattle on the Jones Ranch.

Our other model, Teresa Padgett, fourteen, got her double-registered (AQHA and Palomino) gelding, Gold Alibi, when she was ten. Under the expert supervision of her mother, Carla, Teresa trained "Pal" all by herself. Teresa rides Pal for pleasure and competition, both Western and English.

I met Pat Taylor when I went to his dad's saddlery in Pilot Point to borrow some tack for photos. I ran into him again at a local AQHA show, where I also met Kyle Manion and his mother, Chris Edge. His dad, Tommy Manion, is a noted trainer. Pat and Kyle, both fifteen, are champion competitors.

I appreciate all the help with this book that I got from friendly representatives of the American Quarter Horse Association, American Paint Horse Association, Appaloosa Horse Club and the American Horse Shows Association.

Finally, I owe a big "thank you" to two Jacks. Thanks to Jack Brainard for his support and expertise (and the use of his tack for the photo of mild to severe bits).

Thanks especially to *my* Jack, my beloved and thoughtful husband, who kept our critters and various other things in good shape while I was busy working on this book!

INTRODUCTION

This is a book that you can read on your own and learn the basics of riding stock seat, or Western style. If you want to learn how to select and train the perfect horse, how to build the perfect barn or give your horse a shot without getting kicked, this book won't tell you. You can find that information in other books. You'll also need to look elsewhere for ways to prepare your horse to win cutting, reining or other Western type competitions. There are many books that explain horses from many points of view, and that's the way it should be. But this is the first book I'm aware of that was written especially for a young person who wants to learn how to ride his or her horse Western style.

Before I was old enough to go to school, I knew about horses of all sizes and kinds: pleasure horses, young horses in training and fancy show horses. I would spend hours petting them all, watching and learning their ways. You couldn't convince me those horses couldn't talk! Those that were ridable, I rode (stock seat, hunt seat, saddle seat and bareback), with few adults around to show me how to do something right or to stop me from trying some pretty scary moves.

Not only did I survive, I came out on top . . . most of the time. I realize now that I was extremely lucky. The closest I came to having an instructor was watching the trainers on other horse farms in Texas and on a ranch in Oklahoma. I had to be quiet when I watched, and not ask any questions. Otherwise, I'd be run off. Mostly I was self-taught. I read every horse book that I could find in the libraries. The books were full of technical words, foreign words and rules that were hard to follow, but I read them anyway because I wanted to learn. Walter Farley's books (in the "Black Stallion" series) and other children's classics had as much horse information to offer a person of my age as those very formal how-to books.

Maybe I wasn't entirely self-taught. I suppose the horses were my teachers. I know they were my best friends.

Before I had reached my teens, I was showing the older horses and teaching the younger ones—grooming them and getting them used to a rider. I hated it whenever an adult would smile at my fondness for horses and say that I would grow tired of fooling with horses every day, or that I would outgrow horses as soon as I discovered boys. (Boys who love horses probably hear the same kind of thing.)

Good news: It hasn't happened to me yet!

Because this is a book about riding, I include very little advice on feeding and caring for a horse. If you want to learn about stable management, grooming and care, you'll find a list of books about these and other topics at the end of the book. But I do point out important things to watch for, so that you'll know when your horse (that is, the horse you intend to ride) might be sick or too hurt to carry you around. You wouldn't want to add to your horse's discomfort and, besides, a horse that hurts can be dangerous.

One thing more. "Primo" stands for whatever you actually call your horse. I call Primo "he," but "he" can be a mare as well. I think it's better to have a name than to keep saying "your horse" or "it." A horse is much more than an "it"!

RIDE WESTERN STYLE

CHAPTER 1

First
Impressions

Some people are so eager to get into a book that they skip the Introduction. If that's what you did, you need to turn back and read it before you go any further. Otherwise, among other things, you won't know who Primo is.

After you know who Primo is, you're ready to meet him.

Meeting Primo

How do you meet a horse?

Eye to eye. Walk (never run) to where Primo is standing, and exchange greetings. The easiest way to do this is for Primo to be haltered and tied, or bridled and held. The next best way is for him to be alone and loose in a stall or pen. You might be able to walk up and meet Primo while he's loose in a big pasture, but until he gets to know you, this is not likely. Always approach him so that he sees you coming. Never come up from behind and take him by surprise because, if you do, he will run off. If you really startle him, he might even kick at you.

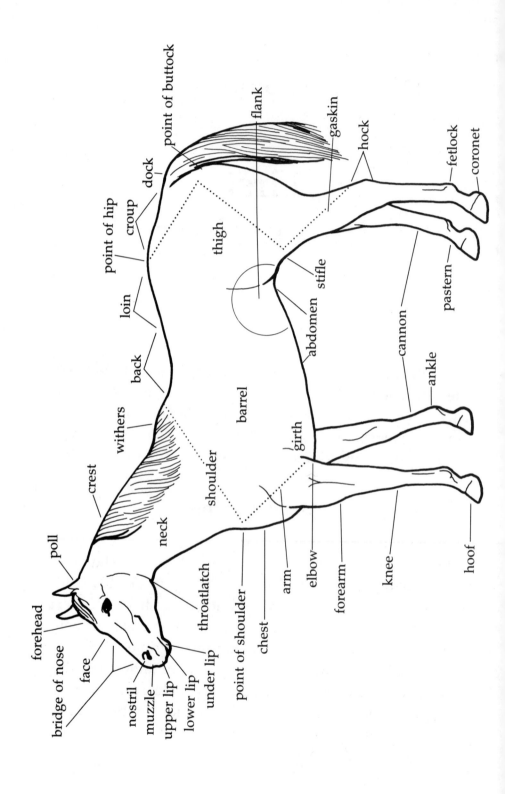

point of buttock
flank
gaskin
hock
fetlock
coronet
dock
croup
point of hip
thigh
loin
stifle
abdomen
back
cannon
ankle
withers
barrel
shoulder
girth
pastern
crest
neck
poll
throatlatch
forehead
point of shoulder
arm
elbow
bridge of nose
chest
forearm
face
knee
nostril
muzzle
upper lip
lower lip
under lip
hoof

2

Primo's Anatomy

The zigzag lines represent bones and joints and show how those in the forequarters line up with those in the hindquarters.

The rump, or hip, is the big apple-shaped part of the hindquarters. The croup is the topline of the rump and ends at the tail. The dock is the smooth underside of the tail. On the hindquarters, the top "zig" line goes from the point of hip to the point of buttock. It "zags" down the thigh to the stifle joint ("elbow"). This connects to the gaskin, or lower thigh. At the other end of the gaskin is the hock ("wrist"), which connects to the cannon.

From here on down, Primo's front and back legs have the same parts. The fetlock, or pastern joint, is at the bottom of the cannon bone. Next is the pastern, then the hoof. The little ridge between the hoof and the pastern is the coronet, or coronary band.

The rounded part of Primo's body is called the barrel. The underside is the belly in front, and the flank in back. The top part under his saddle is his back, and behind that is his loin.

The spine has only three joints capable of up-and-down bending. The "big hinge" (lumbosacral) is between the loin and the hip. The "chest joint" (between the last cervical and first thoracic joints) lets Primo raise and lower his neck, and swing it from side to side. The "head-neck joint" (atlanto axial) lets Primo flex his poll and turn his head.

The withers are the knob above the top "zig" line. The angle where "zig" meets "zag" is the point of shoulder. The chest is in front, between these two points. The "zag" line follows the arm, which is hidden behind heavy muscle. The elbow is visible as a knob behind the forearm (foreleg). The forearm connects to the knee, which connects to the cannon. The top part of Primo's neck (not his mane) is the crest. The poll is where the neck meets the head at the ears. The soft area between the nostrils and above the lip is the muzzle.

Yet Primo wouldn't mean anything "personal" by either act. Running off ("flight") or kicking ("fight") are Primo's responses to what he thinks is a threat to his life. Actually, he wouldn't take time to think. He would simply act on instinct. Flight, fight and other instincts help horses survive in the wild, without any help from people. Horses today have the same survival instincts their ancestors had thousands of years ago.

The best way to greet Primo requires thinking like a horse. Greet him the way horses naturally greet each other when neither one wants to seem a threat. Arrive at his shoulder and stroke his neck first. If he offers his face in a "please scratch me" way, that's what you should do next. Some horses are distrustful and will toss up their heads whenever strangers reach for their faces, while other horses will stick their noses out and nudge a friendly greeting to almost anybody. It all depends on the horse. The point is, your feet stay on the ground until after Primo has had a chance to check you out. This rule for meeting a horse on his terms applies to beginners and experts alike.

How Does Primo Check You Out?

Ideally, he turns his head toward you with both ears in a forward position. His eyes are open, but not so wide that the whites show. He might sniff you and touch you lightly with his muzzle (which will tickle you nicely when he moves it). If so, keep still and let him explore you with his nose and his muzzle (but not with his teeth!). Sometimes he'll even whicker softly. These are all signs that Primo is friendly and curious.

However, if Primo rolls an eye back at you and seems

very tense but doesn't face you, or if he does turn his head but lays his ears back flat and squints his eyes, look out. He's not just checking you out, he's telling you he's annoyed. If Primo acts this way, he is the wrong horse for a rider (of any age) to learn on. He's saying in horse language that he's in no mood to be ridden.

Primo may or may not be saddled and ready for you to ride at this first meeting. It really doesn't matter. What does matter is that you start this relationship right by recognizing Primo as another living creature. He happens to be a horse, but he can become your best friend.

You don't need to bribe Primo with food to win his friendship. All you need to do is speak kindly to him and try not to make any sudden moves. He may not understand what you're saying, but he'll know what you mean from your body language. (We'll talk about this more in Chapter 6.) Meanwhile, there's nothing wrong with giving Primo a piece of carrot or some other treat as a token of friendship. Don't carry food in your pocket. He might smell it and try to take a bite. But he might bite *you* instead!

Once you've introduced yourself to Primo, you may feel a bit uncertain about getting on him. That's all right. It's good that you show healthy respect (even a trace of fear) for an animal who's at least ten times your size. Being afraid from time to time doesn't mean that you won't become a fine rider. The trick is to learn how to *deal* with fear until you can learn the basics of riding. Practically every good rider, and even great ones, must learn to face and overcome fear.

A rider might not start off by being afraid. Sometimes fear doesn't show up until after a person rides well enough to try a more difficult move. Then something goes wrong. Maybe the rider falls off. Sooner or later, rider and horse will part company. But falling off Primo doesn't always mean you'll get hurt. As you'll see in Chapter 5, there are right and wrong ways to fall off a horse.

For now, we'll assume Primo is "tacked up" (meaning, saddled and bridled) and that you've been properly introduced.

What Happens Next?

Well, you don't just get on and ride off into the sunset. Primo has checked you out, now you have to check *him* out. You need an arena or some other enclosed place for this purpose. It should be at least sixty feet wide by seventy-five feet long, and no larger than, say, a baseball diamond's infield. Watch an experienced rider ride Primo first. Pay attention to how this person sits in the saddle and holds the reins. The rider should show Primo's different "gaits" (meaning, ways of moving). For a Western horse, the gaits include the walk, jog and lope. The rider should turn Primo to the right, then to the left, and then stop him. He or she should ride Primo in a circle and back him.

Notice how the rider uses the reins to signal each command. Ask the rider to tell you in advance what the plans are, so you can concentrate more on the rider's moves instead of just watching Primo. Besides watching the rider's hands, see if you can notice any difference in the rider's body or legs, especially when he gets Primo to stop.

One of the first things you need to learn about Primo is how to stop him. Think about your size and Primo's. Now think about Primo's size . . . in motion. (There's a lot of *thinking* involved in good riding.) In Chapters 2 and 5 I'll explain just how you ask a horse to stop.

Why do you *ask*?

Because you are not big enough or strong enough to *force* a horse to stop. For that matter, I've never met an adult who's stronger than a healthy, full-sized horse.

After you've watched Primo being ridden by an experienced rider, and after you've *seen* how this person gets Primo to do everything you plan on doing any time soon, you are ready to get on and find out how it *feels* to ride. Hooray!

First Time on Primo

Before you mount Primo, ask the rider to stay with you. It would be good if that person had a quiet horse to ride to keep you company. If not, he or she can still watch you. You and Primo will probably do just fine. After all, you'll be taking it easy. But at this stage, in case you have a problem, someone else should be nearby.

Now comes the first of many chances you'll have to appreciate the security of a Western saddle as compared to an English saddle. The time will come when you won't need to hold or even touch the saddle horn to keep from falling off. You'll still use the horn, but not for balancing yourself during ordinary moves. Until then, "grab leather" (meaning, grab the horn and any other part of the saddle) whenever you feel you need the support. For Primo's sake, if you need to pull yourself back into balance, *please* use the horn for that purpose instead of the reins! Every time you pull on the reins, the bit they're attached to pulls on Primo's mouth.

Here are some safety measures to follow while learning:

- Wear a safety helmet ("hard hat") or at least a hat that fits your head securely. Also wear boots and long pants. If it's summertime and hot, wear them anyway because they will protect your head, feet and legs.

Western Safety Helmet
Kyle wears a new product, a Western safety helmet. The Western-style hat brim can be removed for cleaning or replacement with another style cover. Or the helmet may be used independently without a cover. (Hat Courtesy of Lexington Safety Products, Inc.)

Also, most shows have rules that require riders to wear helmets or hats.

- Stay in a confined area, with another rider nearby and watching. The rider can be any age, so long as he or she knows horses well enough to help if you need help. After you feel that you can handle Primo without someone right there watching, you will still need to stay in an enclosed area until you can control him, both on and off his back.

- Take your time getting the feel of riding. Don't be in a big hurry to move on. When you do feel ready to ride out in the open, bring along that experienced rider mounted on a sensible horse to help keep Primo relaxed.
- Even when you feel confident about riding out on your own, someone needs to know where you plan to ride and how long you'll be gone, just in case Primo returns to the barn alone.

Meeting Primo
Erin is greeted by C.J., who is held by her grandfather.

Putting the Picture Together

The first thing you do before putting a picture puzzle together is dump all the pieces out of the box and turn the faces up. You use the lines and colors on the faces as well as the shape of each piece as guides to fit it all together.

It's the same with learning to ride.

No matter how carefully you watched Primo being ridden by an experienced rider, a lot of puzzle pieces are still turned down. There's much more to riding than meets the eye, especially when that eye is untrained.

Some folks might consider some of the material in this book too advanced for a beginner, especially a young person, to understand and use. I disagree on two counts. First of all, I think kids are a whole lot smarter than they're given credit for, particularly when it comes to learning about something they enjoy doing. I've seen kids handle college-level information that's clearly presented, and then prove they understand it by using it properly. Second, I think it's better to go a little deeper and learn more facts right away than it is to be lucky but ignorant and pick up bad habits that are hard to break.

CHAPTER 2

Use of Aids

Primo's bridle is used to steer and stop him, and his saddle is there to keep your pants from getting all sweaty and covered with horse hair. To ride Primo, you simply sit in the saddle and use the bridle like handlebars on a bicycle.

Right?

Wrong.

Riding a horse is in some ways like riding a bicycle. Both require good balance. However, you must not put your weight on Primo's reins like you do with your hands on a bike's handlebars. Riding a horse is more like sitting on a bike and coasting. Balance yourself the same way and, if needed, grab leather to keep from falling off Primo while you learn how to control him.

Primo is not a bicycle and he's not a machine, either. You can't just turn him off and on. What we have with a horse and rider is a meeting of two independent minds. When the horse understands what the rider wants him to do, and does it, then the rider has control of the horse.

It's the rider's responsibility to let the horse know what's wanted of him. Nine times out of ten, if the horse fails to do what the rider wants, it's really the rider's fault. The horse, however, usually gets the blame. As Primo's rider, it's your responsibility to give a clear message of what you want him to do. The act of telling Primo what you want him to do is called signaling, or cueing. (Both words mean the same.) Your ways for doing this, for controlling him, are called aids. There are two kinds of aids: natural and artificial.

The Natural Aids

The natural aids for riding are
- hands
- legs
- body
- voice

Hands

Your hands control the reins. Hands are also used to discipline Primo if he does not obey and to praise him with a loving pat after he has done a good job.

The term "good hands" is the standard by which horsemen are rated. Fine riders have good hands, and people who ride horses but are not very good at it do not. We sometimes say they have "no hands."

A horse feels a rider with no hands pull himself into place. That rider uses the reins to pull on the bit instead of using his body and legs to balance himself in place. No-hand fingers are stiff. They don't bend softly. They grip the reins so hard that they don't feel little changes. They're not responsive and they don't "go with" or "give in" to a horse's motions as needed.

Riders with good hands do most of what is needed automatically. They don't have to think first about making their hands be firm or gentle. Good hands are strong, and able to control a horse that would rather not be controlled. Good hands are also sensitive, and able to feel the slightest change through their contact with the rein. Good hands "know" when to apply more pressure and when to ease back. Of course, any rider has to learn what to do with his hands. With lots of practice, "no hands" can become "good hands."

By the way, your arms are included with your hands as being one aid. While you ride, keep your upper arms near your sides and your elbows down, not stuck out and flapping like a chicken's wings in flight.

Legs

Your legs (including your seatbones and your feet) are used to guide and push Primo. They are also used for keeping your own balance.

Here are some experiments that will show what your legs can (or should) do for your riding. (If you don't know the parts of a saddle, see page 31.) If you cannot feel what is described here, try again after you read Chapter 5 and learn about anatomy and the structural differences between boys and girls. Keep working on it. The more strength and sensitivity you develop in your legs, lower back and seatbones, the better you will ride.

First, sit on your hands (slide them under from behind, palms up) and feel your seatbones while keeping your seat muscles as relaxed as possible. Shift ("wiggle") your seatbones side to side. Slide them back and forth. Rotate them (push each foot down, one at a time, like pedaling a bike). Then flex your seat muscles into a tight knot and repeat the same exercises.

After you've done this, stand up and hold your palms (from the front, this time) against your inner thighs (the parts that contact the saddle). Now, without closing your thighs, apply pressure by flexing the muscles that are covered by your hands.

Next, sit in a chair and hold your palms (pointed down from the top) against your calves (the parts that come in contact with the saddle fenders and Primo's sides). Flex your calf muscles by dropping your heels inward and raising your toes outward. Do not move your knees any closer together. You'll be rotating your ankles correctly when the little knobs on the inside of each ankle move toward each other.

Are you surprised at how much power and pressure come from your seatbones and especially your legs? Even if you only weigh fifty pounds, this power and pressure wouldn't surprise Primo. He feels those leg aids, used right or wrong, every time you shift your legs and seatbones. He feels them all the way through a Western saddle, even if you couldn't feel them yourself at first.

Your body is used to guide and drive Primo. You also use your body to "read" Primo (meaning, to pick up his body signals) and to control weight and balance.

It's hard to tell where your seatbones end and the rest of your body begins when it comes to guiding and pushing Primo and reading his next moves. As long as you get the job done, it doesn't matter.

Voice

Your voice is used to encourage and to calm Primo. It is also used to get his attention.

Primo doesn't share our gift of speech, but he communicates well in the language of "feel." He understands the first three aids, hands, legs, and body, better than voice because he can feel them.

We include voice as an aid because Primo understands animallike sounds: clucking, whistling, hissing, barking, and especially growling (our ancestors *and* Primo's finally figured out what those tigers were saying!), and he can learn specific words. Like the other aids, Primo learns voice commands by association. That is, he matches a given sound or word with a given situation. Whether you use sounds or words, or both, always use the same command for the same purpose. Do not change around or use the same sound or word for more than one purpose. For example, "Whoa" is overused. It should be used only to stop Primo. "Easy" could slow him down and "Steady" could get him to relax. Also, avoid words or sounds that sound a lot alike but are intended for entirely different purposes.

"Think-Talk"

Most authorities list only four natural riding aids: hands, legs, body and voice. One more does exist. Known technically as "nonverbal communication," or "visualization," I call this fifth natural aid "think-talk." It's a way for horse and rider to communicate mentally, to exchange information. Think-talk works in the saddle and on the ground. When used on the ground, think-talk is combined with body language, which we'll discuss later.

The idea of think-talk is this: you send Primo a mental picture of what you want him to do. It must be a positive picture, not a negative one. For example, you send a picture of yourself riding Primo away from the corral at a walk and going to a small bush. As you approach the bush, you send a second picture of you and Primo passing it on the right.

These are positive pictures. If you approach the bush sending this picture: "Go around, but *not* to the left," this is a negative picture. To you, this is a tricky way of saying "pass to the right." But Primo cannot envision the negative angle. The picture on his screen doesn't change, or else he "turns off his TV." He's liable to walk right over that bush, assuming it's not a cactus.

Think-talk can work both ways. Primo's message might come across to you as an urge, an unspoken hunch or feeling about something that wasn't already on your mind. For example, if Primo is very thirsty but his good training keeps him from heading to the nearest water hole while he's under saddle, you might come up with the great idea of riding him over to the water hole and letting him drink.

Think-talk doesn't work for everybody. If you're one of the lucky ones, the more you use it the better it works.

The Artificial Aids

The artificial aids for riding include:
- whips
- spurs
- tie-downs
- draw reins

Used correctly, artificial aids are helpful because they reinforce natural aids. Used incorrectly, they can be barbaric!

Whips

The whip (also called a stick, crop, bat, switch or quirt) comes in various sizes and shapes and is used to reinforce (strengthen) any of the natural aids when riding or training

Primo. Sometimes a romal (a braided strip of rawhide attached to the rein) or split rein ends are used as whips.

Use a whip to discipline, *never* to punish. Here discipline is pain given to a horse right after he does something wrong. It's clearly meant to teach "Don't do that!" or to say "I told you to do thus-and-so!" Punishment is pain inflicted for no constructive purpose. Use the whip to discipline immediately, not five minutes later. If it takes you that long to make up your mind whether or not to use it, how can Primo be expected to remember what he did (or did not do) to deserve it?

Spurs

Spurs are fitted onto boots, at the heels, so that they become extensions of leg aids. Spurs should be thought of as two separate aids, one for each foot (actually, leg). Rotate your ankle and drop your heel so that your spur touches Primo's side.

If Primo does not respond to your leg aids, but does for a larger or more experienced rider, then try wearing spurs. Sometimes spurs are the only way for a short-legged rider to make a big horse pay attention to what his or her little feet are saying. A well-timed touch of the spur is *much* kinder to Primo (and gets better results) than constantly kicking him with one or both heels. Use spurs that have blunted mild rowels, not big sharp spikes.

Tie-downs

A tie-down fastens to Primo's bridle. An adjustable strap goes from a band around his nose to be "tied down" by fastening to his saddle girth. Its purpose is to keep him from tossing his head up or stretching his neck out too far. In other words, it restrains him.

Sometimes a horse jerks his head up on purpose to avoid pressure or pain, usually from the bit. Other times he tosses it because he's spirited, nervous or has developed the habit. If head-tossing can be traced back to a rider not using his natural aids properly, then the rider is at fault. The horse may need retraining, but he shouldn't be punished forever by wearing a tie-down. If, however, the horse keeps tossing his head and won't settle down, even though the rider has good hands and does not abuse his mouth with the bit, then that horse needs a disciplinary tie-down.

Most Western performance horses wear tie-downs, but not to make them behave. In barrel racing or roping, for example, a tie-down is used to counterbalance the quickly shifted weight of the horse doing what he's supposed to do.

Simply stated, if you ride Primo mainly for pleasure and both of you behave yourselves, he won't need a tie-down. But if you intend to use Primo for barrel racing or roping, then he will.

Draw Reins

Draw reins are split reins that are run through rings at the end of adjustable straps that fasten on each side of the girth or saddle. This training device is removed after the horse learns to carry his head and neck at a set angle and level. They allow a horse to raise his head only so far (how far depends on how the rider holds the reins). Being a trained horse, Primo probably does not wear draw reins.

You may never need artificial aids for Primo. But if you do, the whip, spurs, tie-down and draw reins are the ones you most likely would use.

Chaps technically are not an aid because they're not used on Primo. But they are an aid in the sense that they can help you hold your position in the saddle. Riding chaps are made of leather, usually suede, for better traction, and are worn over pants. They cover your legs but not your bottom. Most styles are buckled around the waist, then are wrapped around the legs and fastened by long zippers.

Chaps and Spurs
Sunny wears chaps that are too big for her (but they still help) and spurs with rowels of a suitable size.

CHAPTER 3

◄◄◆►►

The Function
of Tack

Tack is what we call bridles, saddles, blankets, halters, lead ropes, tie-downs, boots, leg-wraps and so forth. In other words, any equipment that is worn by the horse for one reason or another. But food for the horse, or medicine, brushes, fly spray, hoof-dressing and shampoo are considered supplies, not tack.

For now, we are only interested in the tack that goes on Primo when you ride him. The most important riding tack is the bridle, and the most important part of the bridle is the bit.

Bits

Many different bits have been used from ancient times to the present. All are merely varieties or combinations of two basic kinds: nonleverage and leverage.

All nonleverage bits belong to the snaffle family. A snaffle bit in its simplest form is a straight bar with a ring at each end to which the rein is attached. A jointed snaffle has two

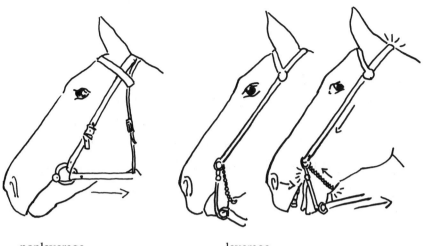

nonleverage
snaffle bit (pulled)

leverage
curb bit (relaxed and pulled)

ring snaffle

low port curb grazing bit

Comparison of Nonleverage and Leverage Bits

When you pull the rein on a snaffle (nonleverage) bit, the pressure goes directly to Primo's tongue. The only other parts affected are the corners of his lips. If the mouthpiece doesn't fit properly, his lips can be pinched by the rings. When you pull the rein on a curb (leverage) bit, however, several parts are affected. The mouthpiece puts pressure on Primo's tongue and on the bars of his gums. If the mouthpiece has a bend in the middle, called a port (a grazing bit being a mild example and a high U-shaped "cathedral spade" being a severe example), this puts pressure on the roof of Primo's mouth. The curb chain puts pressure on his chin. When the portion of the shank above the mouthpiece tilts, this pulls the headpiece down and puts pressure on Primo's poll.

tapered bars that are joined at the center, with rings on the outside ends for the reins.

Leverage bits (curb bits) have a shank at each end of the mouthpiece. A rein is attached to each shank. All leverage bits have curb chains (or straps) that go behind the chin. When you pull on the rein, the shank is tilted and the chain is tightened. This creates a pulley that clamps and squeezes Primo's jaw. (It creates leverage.)

Snaffles fit higher in the mouth than curb bits and they act on the tongue from direct rein pressure. Curbs act on the tongue, bars, chin groove, roof of the mouth and poll.

Gags can be a combination of leverage and nonleverage control. For a snaffle bit gag, the ring at each end of the mouthpiece has top and bottom holes that a cord goes

Snaffle Gag Bit

Sunny uses a direct rein on a snaffle gag bit (also called a draw bit) to ask Rooster to back up. A strong rein pull on the cord could create uncomfortable pressure from all sides. Rooster's mouth stays closed, which shows that Sunny must have good hands.

through. Instead of the rein connecting to the ring, it connects to the cord. The bit still acts on the tongue from direct pressure. But it also creates a squeeze between Primo's mouth and poll because a pull on the rein also pulls on the cord. This pull tightens the headpiece.

Hackamores

The most common gag, the hackamore, has no bit at all. It uses leverage control. There are two kinds of hackamore: mechanical and bosal.

The mechanical hackamore uses a strap or a wrapped chain leverage rig that goes around Primo's jaw and nose. The rig fits into a metal curb shank to which reins are attached. Whenever the reins are pulled, the curb shank is raised and the rig that's fitted around his nose and jaw slides into a tight hold.

A bosal is made of rope, leather strips or a combination of both. The rope's center fits around Primo's nose, then knots at his jaw, and reins are attached to the knot. When the reins are pulled back, the knot presses "Whoa" into the soft jaw area above Primo's chin.

There's a lot of variety possible within the two basic bit groups, depending on how the mouthpieces and shanks are made. Mouthpieces can be designed to give a rider gentle or severe control. The thinner and more irregular the mouthpiece is, the more severe the control will be. Good examples of gentle mouthpieces are a thick, smooth snaffle bit and a curb bit with a low port in the middle (a grazing bit). Shanks are the bars at the ends of the mouthpiece of curb bits to which the reins are tied. The longer the shanks, the more leverage you get by pulling the reins. Therefore, the longer the shanks, the more severe the bit.

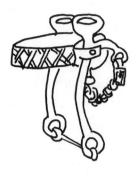

mechanical hackamore

simple bosal hackamore
1. button
2. throat knot
3. heel knot

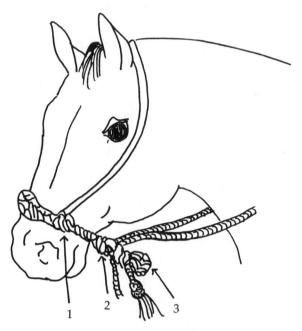

Mechanical and Bosal Hackamores

A mechanical hackamore has three major metal pieces: a U-shaped noseband (with the front part wrapped) and two curving Y-shaped shank pieces (one on each side). The "Y" intersection of each shank piece fits into a sleeve on the nose piece, and is held there by a pin. These pins allow each shank piece to move up and down and side to side. (There's usually a spacer between the shanks, in the rein loops. A strap allows more side to side motion than a metal bar.) The shank piece does more than one job. One "Y" fork holds the curb chain and the other fork holds the headstall, which goes through the slits on top. The "Y" tail serves as a shank for the rein.

When each rein is pulled, its shank piece tilts, and very sensitive parts on Primo are squeezed between the curb chain and noseband. For this reason, a mechanical hackamore should only be used by an experienced rider with good hands.

The bosal hackamore also depends on pressure across the nose and around the jaw, but it is less severe. To be most effective, the bosal should be fitted to Primo so he can feel it move side to side for turn signals and slide up to press "Whoa" at his throat when both reins are pulled. The headstall needs to be as far forward as possible on the

24

bosal for leverage, so that the throat knot can be lifted and give its signal. A "button" on the simple bosal hackamore keeps the headstall from sliding back. The heel knot secures the throat knot, reins and lead rope.

Some bosals also have a fiador, which is more rope knotted and rigged in back of the headstall. The fiador is held in place by a browband added to the headstall. The reins then attach to the fiador, not directly to the bosal.

Bits, Mild to Severe
Left to right, this collection of bits ranges from a mild snaffle to a severe cathedral (bit only, not on a bridle).
1. A plain O-ring snaffle can take Primo back to basics.
2. A broken mouth (snaffle-type mouthpiece) curb with a loose-jawed shank. A loose shank can swivel and will work better than a stiff bit for combination (mainly two-hand) reining. Although the signal is not as sharp for high-tuned neck-reining, this bit is quite comfortable for most horses.

3. A mullen mouth (unbroken) curb with a short loose shank. This is a good move between a broken mouth and a port.

4. A low port curb with loose shank, a good "next step."

5. A low port grazer. The port is wide and low and the shanks are stiff but bent back to allow easy grazing.

6. A medium port curb with a loose medium shank is about the same for Primo as the grazer.

7. A kimberwicke has a curb strap but no shanks. This one has a sliding D-ring and a mild port.

8. A pelham has two sets of reins. One goes to the mouthpiece, usually either a mullen or a mild port like the kimberwicke. A second set of reins goes on the shanks. This loose-jawed pelham with medium shanks helps teach a horse that has only worked on a snaffle to respond to a curb.

9. This is a cathedral ("half-breed") curb with a roller. It has long stiff shanks with a connecting bar. This bit should *only* be used by a very experienced rider on a finished horse.

The list goes on, but you get the idea. Horses are individuals. They differ in many respects, including how their mouths are designed and how they react to the different bits. Riders are individuals also, and they use bits differently. In an expert's hands, one bit can do wonders, while in other hands it can be annoying or even torture.

Which Bit Is Right for Primo?

For a while, at least, it's best to keep Primo on the same bit he was wearing when you first started riding him. As long as the bit (or hackamore) does the job, there's no reason to change. You'll see how to use the bit correctly in the section How Reins Are Used in Chapter 5.

A beginning rider of any age should not ride a green horse that is also learning. A green horse is a challenge even for an experienced rider. A rider who doesn't know exactly how to ask for something can confuse the horse so much that the horse either explodes or gives up trying to do anything at all. If Primo is a finished, or made, horse (meaning he's fully trained), he'll neck-rein and use some kind of leverage bit. He'll likely use a mild grazing curb or maybe a hackamore because, for Western horses, snaffles are mainly training bits. Since Primo was trained first in a snaffle bit, you might want a snaffle for his second bit. Wait, however, until you are confident with neck-reining Primo before you use a snaffle on him. You'll hold the reins two-handed for using a snaffle and one-handed for neck-reining with a curb. Some show classes have rules that restrict the kind of tack you can use, so know the rules before you enter Primo in an event. If you have to change bits before showing Primo, do not wait until right before the show. Give him plenty of time—measured in weeks, not hours—to get used to a new bit.

Small differences, such as smooth or twisted wire mouthpieces that are otherwise the same size and weight, do not change the bit's basic action. Major factors are

- The mouthpiece's size (how big around and how long).
- Its shape (including the port in the middle).
- Its taste (differs according to what it's made of).
- How long the shank is.
- Whether the shank is made as one piece with the mouthpiece or is loose (so that it slides or bends).
- The shape of the shank (how it's bent and angled).
- How long the *other* end of the shank is (the end that connects to the headpiece, not to the reins).
- The overall weight and balance of the bit (plus the added weight and balance of the reins).

Some bits seem better suited to particular duties. People who specialize in performance activities like cutting, reining and barrel racing are finicky about the bits they use on their horses. You'll learn about these favorite bits should you get involved in the activities yourself or perhaps you'll read magazine articles that discuss them. If Primo's bit fits right but it still won't work, try something else. But don't switch to a new bit and expect instant success. Sometimes a change can do wonders, however. If you run into a problem with bits, tell your vet about it the next time he or she examines Primo. The vet may be able to solve the problem without your having to change Primo's bit. The problem could be with his teeth.

Different Styles of Reins

Reins are attached to the bit so that you and Primo can communicate through the bit. Reins can be leather, nylon (plain or plastic-coated), rubber-coated leather or nylon, cotton or horsehair. They can be braided, even silver-plated, or just a simple rope.

A closed rein is one continuous rein. A roping rein is a closed rein that is adjustable in length (usually short to very short). Some closed reins snap onto one or both sides of the bit and are easiest to remove and change. Others must be buckled or laced on. Sometimes a long braided rawhide strip (romal) is attached to the center of a closed rein. Romals are considered part of the California-style of Western riding.

Split reins are two separate reins, one off each side of the bit. Each rein is about as long as a roping rein (about seven feet).

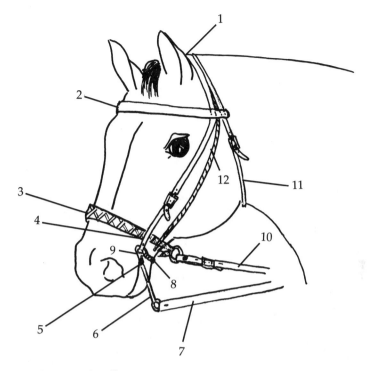

Parts of the Headstall

1. crown
2. browband
3. tie-down noseband
4. cheek piece
5. mouthpiece end
6. curb bit shank
7. rein

8. curb chain
9. upper shank and bit ring (attaches to cheek piece)
10. tie-down strap
11. throatlatch strap
12. tie-down headpiece

Parts of the Headstall

The headstall is the bridle without the reins.

The headpiece is the part that goes over the head at the poll and attaches to the bit or hackamore. You could get by with using nothing more than a single headpiece, a bit and the reins. But if your bit is a leverage type, you would need to add a curb chain or strap (or a combination). Most headpieces have cheek pieces that buckle onto the crown (top) portion on one end and the bit on the other. Cheek pieces allow the length of a headpiece to be adjusted. This is helpful for fitting the bit properly. Next, you need some way to keep the headpiece in place. Otherwise, when the headpiece slips backward (which it will do, unless anchored) the bit will become too tight. Sliding forward is no problem. Primo's ears keep that from happening. The simplest way to keep the headpiece from slipping back is to use an ear loop. A sliding ear loop is attached to the headpiece and slides to fit over either ear. On a one-ear or split-ear headstall, one side of the headpiece is already shaped into a split for the ear to be slipped through.

Another way to keep the headpiece in place is to use a browband. Made either to match the headpiece or to add color, the browband crosses Primo's face right under his ears. It has two sets of loops—a larger one for the headpiece to pass through and a smaller pair right behind. That's where the narrow chin strap passes through to become part of the headpiece. The chin strap keeps the headpiece from accidentally being pulled off over Primo's ears.

These are the basic parts of a bridle. All sorts of extras can be added, such as the tie-down and draw reins we discussed in the Artificial Aids section. Study the reason for whatever you might add. Then ask yourself, "Who really needs this? Primo or me?" If the answer is yourself, you should work on improving your riding instead of putting an extra burden on Primo.

Saddles

The stock-seat saddle was designed to carry a rider working stock (cattle). The cowboy had to sit in his saddle all day long, day after day, and be comfortable. His horse needed

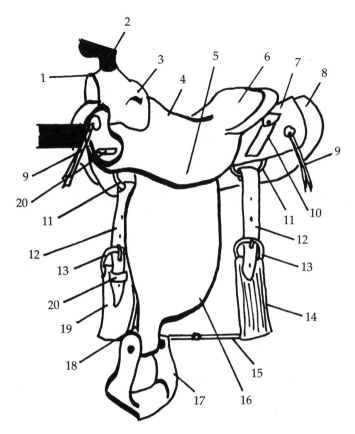

Parts of a Stock Seat Saddle (Full Rig)

1. pommel (front part of any saddle)
2. horn (top of stock seat pommel)
3. fork (ridge part of pommel)
4. seat
5. seat jockey (flap)
6. cantle (back part of any saddle seat)
7. upper flank skirt
8. skirt
9. strings (longer if used to tie on gear)
10. scabbard (optional, for knife or hoof pick)
11. D-rings (also attached to rigging straps)
12. girth straps, or latigos (can be longer)
13. girth rings, buckle style (If there is no buckle, loop girth strap between girth ring and D-ring, then tie strap.)
14. back girth
15. connecting strap (connects front and back girths)
16. fender
17. stirrup
18. stirrup leather (under fender, for adjusting stirrup length)
19. front girth
20. strap keepers (two styles, both serve the same purpose)

to be comfortable, too. But the cowboy did more than move cattle from one place to another and guard the resting herd. His other duties involved hard riding, so bursts of speed, quick turns and hard stops were common. He needed a saddle that would support him during all this riding and also carry supplies for himself and his horse.

Today's stock-seat saddle satisfies all those original needs and more. The saddles have become specialized. They come in eight different basic styles:

1. Pleasure (for pleasure, used by the casual rider)
2. Ranch (a throwback to the original working saddle)
3. Roping (extra sturdy, built to handle cattle)
4. Cutting (flat seat allows the rider to sit deep and close to the horse's back and follow his "diving" movements)
5. Reining (Western "dressage" saddle, holds the rider in an ideal balance to follow the horse's movements)
6. Barrel racing (built for speed, to support the rider on the straightaway and around sharp turns)
7. Show (larger, fancier version of a pleasure saddle)
8. Equitation (similar to show saddle, but the seat and stirrups are designed to give the rider a "good seat").

Many of today's Western youth saddles are light, for example, twenty to thirty pounds, compared to forty to fifty pounds for an adult-size saddle. Although lighter, they are very strong. This is because of improved "trees." Trees are "saddle skeletons" to which leather or other materials are added. In general, a saddle's seat is either flat (so the rider can slide forward or back) or built up (padded higher in front, so the rider has less sliding room but more comfort). Seat, skirts and fenders, fork, horn, cantle, stirrups (plus leathers) and rigging are basic equipment. But they come in many different shapes, and also in different fabrics. Leather is still used primarily, although synthetics are gaining in popularity. Leather or leatherlike fabrics show either the rough side or the smooth side and are stitched. They can also be carved or plain and even silver-plated.

The stock saddle's basic styles of rigging have changed very little. (Rigging is what keeps the saddle in place on Primo's back.) For all styles, a strap goes in front of the tree at the pommel and another one just behind the cantle. Rings are attached to these two straps. To these rings another strap is added. This other strap, called a girth, or cinch, fastens the saddle to Primo. (*Girth* and *cinch* mean the same thing. Which name is used depends on where you live.) Each style puts the girth in a different place on the saddle.

Here are the two styles of rigging:

1. A double-rigged, or full-rigged (again, both mean the same), saddle uses two girths. The front girth is cinched tighter than the back girth. (Used this way, *cinch* means "fasten.") Many modern full-rigged saddles are actually only seven-eighths rigged. The front girth is set back slightly, perhaps a couple of inches, more or less.

2. A three-quarter-rigged saddle uses one girth that is not as far forward as the front girth on a full-rigged saddle. Most youth pleasure saddles are three-quarter rigged.

Which style you use depends on two things: how you ride and how Primo is built. For pleasure riding, you won't need a full-rigged saddle. You should have no problem changing Primo from a full-rigged saddle to one with a single girth, but the opposite is not true. That extra girth can upset him.

A full rig will stay in place without having the girths cinched up uncomfortably tight. But the front girth can rub a painful sore just behind the long elbow of a horse with steep shoulders (meaning, shoulders that are more up-down than slanting). A seven-eighths rig would take care of this

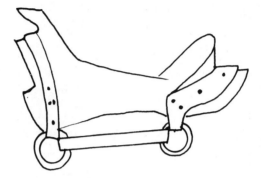

Full-Rigged Tree

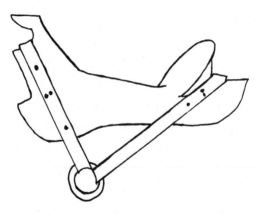

Three-quarter Rigged Tree

Stock Seat Rigging Styles

Straps are anchored to the front and back of the saddle tree for either style. For a fully rigged saddle, two rings (for two girths) go on each side. For a three-quarter rigged saddle, one ring is positioned on each side where it will provide the best balance for using just one girth. After the basic rigging is attached to the tree, leather and the various trimmings are added.

problem. Two girths keep the saddle from tipping up in back when weight shifts to the front. This happens in quick stops or when a calf or steer is on the other end of a rope that's attached to the horn. A full rig can be dangerous in the hands of someone who forgets to unfasten the back girth before the front girth when removing the saddle. Anytime the back girth is too tight around his flanks—which is what's done to rodeo bucking horses to make them buck—Primo might show you he can "rodeo," too!

What if the back girth is fastened to fit, but later slides back around Primo's rounded belly to his flanks?

This is similar to a headstall sliding back and making the bit too tight. Just as an ear piece keeps the bit in place on a bridle, a spacer strap is attached between girths to keep the back girth in place.

Any saddle can slip backward on Primo when you ride up steep hills, unless you use a breast strap. A breast strap is a broad strap, or two straps with a ring in the center that fits across Primo's chest. Smaller straps fasten the breast strap to each side of the saddle's rigging. Think of a breast strap as a pair of suspenders that keep the saddle from sliding back or over to one side. You can see when and why it is useful. It must fit properly, however, and not be too loose or too tight.

A Saddle to Fit Both You and Primo

Saddles come in different sizes to fit the rider. In order for you to ride well and be comfortable, the saddle must fit you. If it's too big, you'll slide around. If it's too small, you will be pinched and unable to settle into a deep seat. Given a choice between a saddle that's too big and one that barely fits and is nearly too small, take the larger one so that you can develop a deep seat. If it's just a little too big, mainly in the stirrups, you can adjust it for now and grow into fitting it better later.

Saddles are sized according to how long the seat is. Children's (youth) saddles go from ten inches through fourteen inches. Twelve inches is the most common size. The adult's saddles range from fourteen and a half inches to eighteen inches or more. Finding the correct size involves more than admitting how big or small your buttocks are. The length of your legs must also be considered. If your legs are short, you need a smaller size because your seat just doesn't sit back as far on Primo as the seat of someone with long legs. A saddle's seat angle and its padding also affect how it fits the rider.

All saddles have stirrups that are generally the right width for the feet that will go in them, and the leathers are adjustable in length. Some stirrups have coverings (called hoods, or tapaderos) attached in front to keep your feet from going in too far, and for protection while riding in heavy brush.

Any saddle that you intend to use needs a "sit test" first. The test doesn't have to be on a horse. A steady rack that's strong enough to support you and the saddle will do just fine. You need to find the right seat length and, because Primo's size will cause some changes, the right width.

Mainly, this is your chance to make sure the stirrups and fenders are hung at an angle that is comfortable for your legs. It's important to check that your legs don't feel cramped when your feet are in the stirrups and that the stirrups hang at an angle that gives you freedom to swing your feet freely and rotate your ankles.

The saddle doesn't need to be new. A used saddle in good condition can be a real bargain. But even when a saddle is new and the leather still a bit stiff, you can tell if the fenders and stirrups are in line with how *you* are in line. If they are not, your knees and ankles will be stuck in a strained position and can be rubbed raw where they contact the fenders and stirrups.

If you already own a saddle that you're unhappy with, you can make it more comfortable by having the fenders and stirrups adjusted so that they hang right for *you*. *Do not try to reset them yourself* by a method called "rolling" the fenders. This is a way of permanently changing the set of the leather fibers, as the saddlemaker did to cover the tree. If you make a mistake, you'll end up with fenders and stirrups that are even more uncomfortable than before. It's too easy, for instance, to turn one stirrup just a little more than the other when you roll and set the leather. Riding in a saddle that has this problem is not just a matter of being uncomfortable. It's more like being miserable!

Find out where other riders take their saddles for repairs and adjustments. Take your saddle to the place that gets the best recommendations.

The saddle must fit Primo comfortably, too. Otherwise, he will get a sore back that will cause problems for both of you. A saddle's basic fit depends on its tree. How wide and how long it is, how far back the pommel is and its skirts are all factors. Saddles that are too wide, too narrow or too long can pinch or rub Primo. They also won't distribute weight evenly over his back. You can make minor changes by using the right pad under the saddle. If Primo already has a sore back, a special pad can give relief. Even if the saddle fits perfectly, always use a pad and/or a blanket.

Leg Equipment and Ropes

Galloping boots and other leg equipment are designed to protect or support Primo's legs. They can do more harm than good unless you know what you're doing. Don't use any leg equipment on Primo unless a vet or other horse expert tells you what he needs, and why. Then get this expert to show you how and when to use the leg equipment.

Ropes used for working cattle are stiff and have nooses at one end. Ropes used for this purpose vary considerably. You would need an expert's help here. Meanwhile, you'll use other ropes and lines on Primo. A lead line is used to lead and then tie Primo. It's about ten feet long and has a snap and sometimes a chain at one end. A trailer tie is a short rope with snaps at both ends and is used to tie a haltered horse in the trailer or to it.

Care of Tack

For the sake of your safety and Primo's comfort, take care of your tack. Dirt, moisture, Primo's shed hair and sweat must be removed, or your nice flexible tack will soon become stiff and uncomfortable.

Take your bridle, breast collar, tie-down and other tack apart completely on a regular basis. Check for weaknesses. Examine the leather for rot and the buckles for metal fatigue. Give your saddle a thorough going-over as well. If something breaks while you're riding, the results can range from inconvenient and embarrassing to downright dangerous. Although no tack will last forever, it'll last far longer (sometimes years longer) with proper care than without it.

Washable tack, such as saddle pads, nylon bridles, cinches, halters and lead lines, can be hosed off and maybe even tossed in the washer. Leather requires special care because it's an animal product that's porous and, broadly speaking, still alive. The protein in leather needs a "diet of fat" (lubricating) in order to allow the fibers to slide across one another so the leather can be flexible.

Leather can be ruined by three things: too much moisture, too much dryness and the salt in Primo's sweat. Both water and dryness remove the leather's vital fats and oils. Water melts or washes the oils out. Dryness causes the oils to evaporate, especially when you use heat to dry wet leather in a hurry instead of letting it dry naturally. Salt deposits from Primo's sweat block the leather's pores.

After your ride (and after you've taken care of Primo), treat wet or sweaty tack to remove dirt. First, gently brush or use a dry towel to rub off as much mud and sweat as possible. Clean and dry the metal parts, too. Rinse the leather with a barely damp (not dripping wet) sponge. Next, coat both sides of the leather (not the bit, however) with glycerine soap. Glycerine soap contains fats and oils that are recommended for cleaning and preserving leather goods. It comes as a bar or in liquid form. Do not add water. Either rub a bar of soap directly against the leather or spread liquid glycerine soap over all the surfaces.

Whenever the leather feels dry, maybe once a month, apply an oil preservative. Any animal or vegetable oil (even cooking oil) will do, but avoid mineral oil (even a mixture of it). It can harden leather and rot the stitching. Do not use soap or oil on suede or rough-out leather. Soap and oil will ruin the nap. Your local tack or feed store has special products for cleaning this kind of leather.

Store your tack in a dry place. Leather will grow mold and mildew if left very long in a damp place. Protect all of your tack from dust by covering it or storing it. Do not put leather tack in a plastic bag. It needs to "breathe."

CHAPTER 4

---◆---

Making
Tiger Stew

An old recipe for making tiger stew describes a lot of mouth-watering ingredients that go into the stew, and then it says, "But first, you must catch the tiger." Riding is great fun, but first, you must catch Primo.

Catching Primo

As a trained horse, Primo should be easier to catch than a tiger. As you found out when you first met Primo, the secret of getting along with a horse is to think like one. That means to see things that go on between you from his point of view.

Before you go after Primo, think about:

- Where he is and what you'll need to take with you.
- Making contact with him.
- Putting the halter and/or lead rope on him.
- Leading him (maybe just around the corral).

- Doing something with him, even if you only pet him as a reward before turning him loose again.

Most of the time, you'll catch Primo to ride him. If you want him to look forward to being caught, catch him sometimes just for a treat and not to ride him. For example, you might lead him to a nice patch of grass, then brush him while he eats it. And I'm sure you'll enjoy spending plenty of time with Primo without even trying to catch him.

As long as you stay calm and confident, you can usually approach any horse accustomed to people. A horse can be trained to come when he's called, even if he's grazing in the middle of a pasture. He'll approach the trusted person who called him and let that person halter him. If not, he'll at least stand still for someone to walk up and slip the lead rope around his neck in case he tries to leave before the halter goes on. Primo might let you come up and halter him in the pasture. However, it's better for you to start out by catching him in a corral or stall. It's also smart to have someone quietly nearby.

Approach his shoulder, just like you did when you met him for the first time. If he already wears a halter, ease your hand up his neck, calmly grab the halter and snap on the lead rope.

You may want to keep a halter on Primo until you and he get used to each other, but once he's settled in, remove it. Halter Primo only when you want to lead or tie him. Otherwise, he could get himself tangled and hurt or become frightened.

If Primo would rather play games when you want to catch him, you'll want to read Chapter 9 to get a better understanding of the horse's ways.

Leading Primo

To lead Primo, hold the lead line firmly about a foot from where it snaps onto the halter. Never wrap the lead around your hand. Then face the direction you want to go, and start walking. Primo should move calmly and keep up with you. His shoulder will be in line with your hip or else right behind it, so you might try to match your steps with his. Horses are usually led from their near side. In other words, Primo would be on your right and you'd be on his left as you lead him. However, Western horses are taught to lead from either side, so it's a good idea to lead Primo from his far side sometimes to keep him in practice.

Don't try to get Primo to come along by facing him and pulling him toward you. If he's a cow pony, Primo might back up and try to hold you like a calf on the end of his rope. He'll also back up if he's afraid or just stubborn. It's simply more natural for a horse (also a dog) to follow someone who faces the same direction he's moving in rather than follow someone who is facing him and walking backward. So if you suspect Primo is being stubborn, avoid turning around and giving him a "Now, listen here!" lecture. This only makes matters worse. Losing your temper never helps. Pulling on the rope is a mistake, too, because Primo is stronger than you are.

If Primo seems glued to the ground, what can you do?

Hold the lead rope with your outside hand. (If you're on Primo's near side, that would be your left hand.) Then reach your inside (right) hand behind you and use it to slap him on his arm. Say "Giddup" or whatever, give a quick tug on the rope and step forward. If a slap of the hand alone doesn't faze Primo, add the end of the lead rope to your slap. If he still won't move forward, try taking a step or two to the right or to the left. A step to the right is better, because you can add a nudge to his arm or shoulder with your hip or elbow without turning. Then, as soon as he's moved either way, straighten up and continue walking forward.

If you have the opposite problem, and Primo wants to take off with you, lean back and try to hold on to the rope. Once Primo learns he can break away from you, you'll probably need an experienced horseman to convince him not to do it every time he pleases. Should Primo lash out or drag you off your feet, *drop the rope!* Your safety always comes first. If he gives you warning by acting snorty and spirited, jerk hard on the lead rope and speak a sharp, "Stop it!" Then immediately try to relax him. Do not walk on until Primo seems settled down. Probably he didn't intend to misbehave, he just forgot about you while instinctively reacting to something. He'll calm down sooner if you stay calm (or at least act calm).

If Primo wears no tack, you'll need to carry it along when you approach him. This should present no problem, provided you don't make a big production of it. Have the lead rope already snapped to the halter and the halter already unbuckled so you can slip it on easily. Coil the rope neatly so that it won't get tangled or drag along on the ground. You can give Primo a hug and grab him if both hands are free. Carry the halter and lead rope looped over your shoulder until you reach Primo, then free yourself. *Never* knot the rope around your waist.

This is a good time to use think-talk. Think "Primo will let me go up and put a halter on him." Once you've made contact with Primo, reach around his neck from underneath and give him a nice hug. Just don't stand where he can easily step on your feet! After you've hugged him a while and maybe rubbed his neck or whatever he wants you to

Haltering Primo

Cyrus carries the halter and lead rope on his shoulder. This leaves both hands free so he can give Bo a hug-hold.

Keeping contact with Bo, Cyrus gets the lead rope over Bo's neck to hold him, just in case.

Cyrus puts the halter on and fastens it.

Cyrus is in good position to lead Bo, who follows willingly. Note how Cyrus carries the excess line in his other hand. He keeps a good grip, but he does *not* wrap the excess line around his hand.

rub, stay where you were when you hugged him and ease the rope around his neck. Next put on the halter. Then praise him. Haltering can be a pleasant experience for both of you.

If you approach Primo with a positive "I'm the boss but I'm a friendly boss" attitude, catching him should be no problem.

Tying Primo

Most of the time, you will lead Primo someplace and tie him in order to groom him and tack up (put the saddle and bridle on him). Make sure that whatever you tie him to is solid. A post or ring designed specifically for this purpose is ideal. Don't tie him to flimsy things, such as a door handle or a fence rail or a dead tree branch. One good jerk from an average-size horse could rip something loose, leaving the poor beast tied to something that frightens him and "chases" him while he runs for dear life. Use a lead rope with a halter or neck strap, or a rope tied around his neck to tie Primo. *Never* use the reins for this purpose. He could pull back and break a rein or injure his mouth with the bit.

Having found a suitable place to tie Primo, what kind of knot should you use?

Always tie a horse by some kind of quick-release knot that can be untied by a pull from *you*, not him. Should Primo rear or sit back in a panic and put all his weight against his end of the rope, you obviously could not loosen that end to untie the knot. With a quick-release knot, Primo can pull on his end until he quits or the rope breaks. Yet all you need to do to get him untied is to jerk on the other end. Study the drawings of a half-hitch, also called a slip knot. It's the easiest of several quick-release knots. Use a length of rope to practice tying and releasing half-hitches.

Figure 1

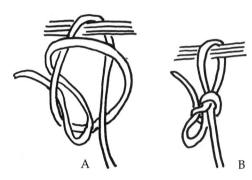

A   B

Figure 2

Half Hitch Knot—Two Versions

Figure 1 works well with a soft lead line. This shows the half hitch before it is pulled tight. Tighten it by pulling on the end that Primo's attached to. Release it by pulling on the other end (the tail end).

To make a fancy half hitch "chain," fold another loop in the tail end, fairly close to the first hitch, then stick that loop through the big outside loop. Don't pull it tight. It'll hold. Make adjustments so your chain loops are the same size. Keep making loops until you have just enough rope for a short tail.

Figure 2 works better when using stiff material. The drawing on the left is "loose," so you can see how to tie the rope. The drawing on the right shows it tightened. The only difference between the knots in figures 1 and 2 is that the figure 2 knot has an extra wrap before you pull the loop through. Release it the same way. *Pull on the tail end.* (If you're left-handed, you may have to reverse the directions. The knot will look different but it will work the same quick-release way.)

After you've tightened the knot (either way), you can drop the tail end through the loop for extra security. But you'll have to pull it back out before you can pull it to release the knot.

When you tie Primo and don't want him to graze, tie him high (at least as high as his withers). Leave slack in the rope so he can move his head, but not enough for him to reach the ground. If you intend to stake him out to graze, tie him very low, so he won't be as likely to get his body and legs tangled in the rope. Then keep your eye on him in case he does.

Your careful planning can usually prevent Primo from getting tangled. But if it happens anyway, untie him as quickly and calmly as you can. The calmer you stay, the less excited he will become. Unless he's wrapped so tightly that pain makes him panic and struggle, Primo probably won't move until you get him loose. But, if worse comes to worse and you can't get him untied or untangled (and you don't have a pocketknife to cut the line), stay well away from his thrashing hooves and go for help.

A panic snap is great for controlling Primo's safety when he's tied, especially on a trailer tie. In an emergency, a panic snap is faster and more foolproof than a quick-release knot (particularly one that might have been tied wrong). Hook the panic snap onto one of the trailer's rings. Then, when you unhook Primo, he'll have a lead line.

Another way to lead and especially to tie Primo is with a neck strap and an overhead line. They may not be typical Western tack, but I like them and often use a strap instead of a halter. I make my horses' neck straps, using flat nylon line (also called webbing), rings and panic snaps. Anyone who sews can study the photo and make a neck strap.

The advantage of a neck strap is that it can stay on without getting in the way of the bridle. The advantage of an overhead line is that it gives both you and your horse freedom to move around. If the overhead line is tied to a sturdy

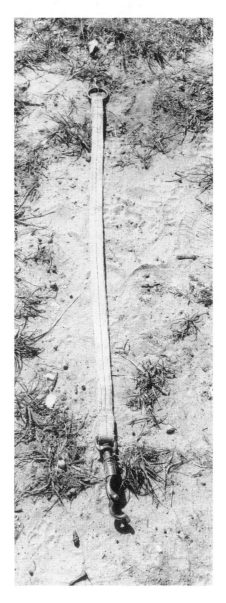

Neck Strap

This is a neck strap, laid out flat. To make one for Primo, measure around his neck about three inches below his ears and cut some flat nylon line twice that length. Burn both ends to seal them and to keep them from unraveling. String a panic snap through one end and a ring through the other end. Fold so that the ends of the strap meet in the center. Then sew the lines together as one piece (twice as thick, in other words).

branch out far enough from the tree's trunk (or post or wall, if tied to a beam in a barn), Primo could turn a complete circle or you could circle him without either of you getting trapped.

Neck Strap on an Overhead Line
When the snap and ring are added to the line, it becomes long
enough to slide farther down Primo's neck than the original three
inches below his ears. My horse Spock is hooked by his neck strap to
an overhead line wrapped around a tree limb. Note the slack line and
the panic snaps.

Tacking Up

Once you've caught Primo and tied him with the idea of
riding him, you need to groom him. A handy grooming tool
is a rubber massage curry, especially one that fits nicely in
your hand. Its rounded teeth give Primo a massage while it
lifts out dirt and loose hair. You'll need at least one brush,
also. Primo's legs and face need delicate strokes, but grooming the rest of him properly should be a real workout for
you. Watch Primo's response as you groom him. (Chapter
9 tells you how to read his responses.) He'll tell you which

parts are sensitive and which parts he likes to have massaged.

I won't describe in detail how to groom Primo here, but I will mention these important things: Clean his feet and check for loose or missing shoes. Brush the dirt from where the saddle and other tack will go. Dirt under his pad or girth

Checking Primo's Front Foot

Get close to Primo's shoulder and hold his front foot between your legs, just above your knees. This leaves both hands free to work. Protect your back from strain by keeping it as straight as possible. Pretend that you are sitting on a stool.

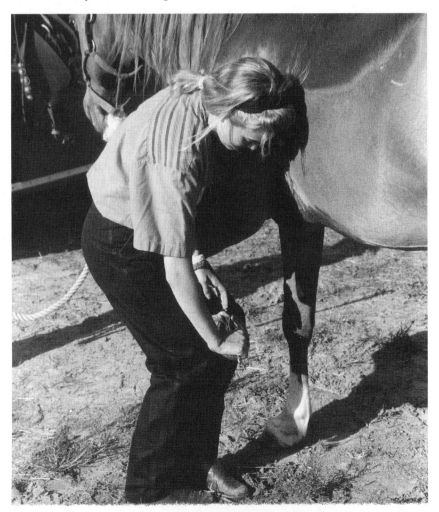

Checking Primo's Back Foot

Again, position yourself next to Primo. This time, let his back foot rest on your knees. Tuck his hock under the arm next to him. If he's too big for you to get your arm over his hock and still leave both hands free to check his foot, do the same thing *beneath* his hock, along his cannon. Either armpit grip makes him more secure. When Primo feels secure, he's less likely to try to pull his foot free.

feels to Primo like pebbles in your shoes do to you. After grooming him, you are ready to tack him up. As a rule, you'll saddle him before you bridle him.

What difference does it make which you do first?

Usually, you'll tie Primo by the halter, and the halter

comes off before the bridle goes on. So you'd want to keep him haltered until you've done everything except bridle him.

The Saddle

Here is how you saddle Primo:

• Position the pad on Primo's back so that it is slightly forward of where it will eventually sit. Check that the sides are even.

• Before you lift the saddle into place, be sure the girth and straps (latigos) are secured to their carriers. Hook the far-side stirrup over the horn, too, so there's less chance of moving the pad when you lift the saddle up on to Primo's back.

• Speaking calmly to Primo, stand at his near side, on a sturdy mounting block if necessary. Raise the saddle up high enough to get its far side across Primo's back without moving the pad, center it, then ease it down squarely onto the pad. Do not just plop it down!

If using a blanket, smooth out any wrinkles because they can cause saddle sores. Then reach your fingers under the blanket at the center, from both ends, and lift it up slightly into the little hollow area on the saddle's underside. A blanket that's too tight and then held down that way by the saddle can rub sores on Primo's shoulders.

• Gently jiggle both pad and saddle (as one piece) to get it all settled. Then work it back so that the pommel rests right behind Primo's withers. If the saddle is too far forward, Primo won't have the freedom to move his forearms. If it's too far back, you'll be sitting behind his center of balance instead of over it.

• Go around to the far side and release the stirrup and girth. Be sure the girth isn't twisted.

Using a Block to Reach Primo
An overturned washtub makes a handy block when you need help reaching Primo's back with the saddle or to get on him.

• Come back and, before tightening the girth, hook the near-side stirrup over the horn to get it out of your way.

Anytime you move around Primo at close quarters, while tacking up or whatever, be careful not to startle him. One way to let him know where you are is by *feel*. Give him a pat, then keep your hand in contact with him and just slide it around as you pass in front of or behind him to get to the other side.

• Reach under Primo's belly, grasp the girth and bring it up so you can run the strap through it.

This would be the most likely time for you to discover that you've placed the saddle too far back. If so, you'll need to remove both the saddle and the pad, and start over. Never slide the pad forward, because this can push Primo's body hairs forward to pinch him and cause problems. (*Note*: An experienced rider can see if the saddle is placed right. He or she can then show *you* how to tell, both by the saddle's position and by how far back the girth is, usually four inches from Primo's elbow. Until you get the hang of things, don't be shy or embarrassed about asking someone for help.)

• Now tighten the girth (for a full rig, the front girth). This can be done in one of two ways.

1. If your girth has a tongued buckle and your strap has holes to fit the buckle, tighten it as you would a regular belt. This is the easiest way to fasten the girth, but not always the best way, because a "just right" fit for Primo might be beyond the last hole or between two holes.

2. In most cases, the strap is wrapped back and forth from the rigging ring to which it's attached (the D-ring) and the girth buckle, then tied at the D-ring. It's easier to understand by studying the photos of tying a girth. Keep the knot loose until you've gone back and worked out the slack. Pull the strap tight, then pull the knot tight. Finally, tuck the strap's end through the carrier so it won't flap around.

For a full rig, do the back girth next. It should be tight enough to just barely touch Primo's belly. You know why you shouldn't pull it too tight, but leaving it too loose is also

Saddle Too Far Forward
This saddle and pad are placed too far forward. Don't be fooled by the girth strap. It's being held at a slant. You can't see what will happen when it has been drawn snug and straight. Look at the front skirt and the pommel, and then look down at Rooster's front leg. There's no room left for the girth.

Saddle Too Far Back
Again the strap is slanted. But imagine it already drawn snug and then look at the front skirt and pommel. This time, the saddle is set too far back. The girth would go at least six inches behind Rooster's elbow.

Tying the Saddle's Girth

The strap is passed through the girth's ring from behind and pulled out in front. This girth is padded for the comfort of the horse. It also has a buckle and the strap has holes. If the strap has a hole in just the right spot, you can put the buckle tongue in the hole, secure the excess strap through the keeper and be done.

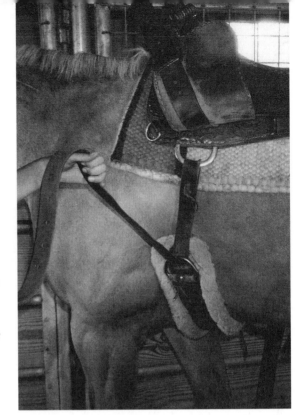

To tie a knot, first pass the strap through the girth buckle and the D-ring twice. Set up the knot as shown here. Next, push the strap end down under the crossover. Work out any slack, then pull on the strap end to draw the knot down flat. Finally, put the strap end through the keeper so it won't flap.

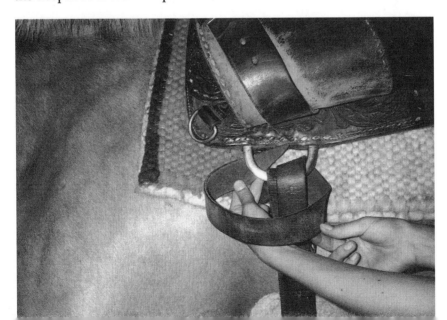

bad. Primo could kick at a fly and get his foot caught in a floppy girth. Check the spacer strap, and unbuckle the back girth first when unsaddling.

Good habit: When unsaddling, before you take the saddle off, grab about halfway down the girth strap. Use this as an "end" and draw the strap halfway again through the ring for neat storage. Also, secure the girth by its buckle to the far side.

• If you use a breast collar, it will attach to rigging rings on both sides of the saddle. When used with a tie-down, it will attach to a ring at Primo's belly on the girth. For regular use with that saddle, the collar stays buckled to the far side ring. Bring the collar across Primo's chest. Be sure it is centered (look at its center ring), then buckle the near side. If the collar needs tightening or loosening, adjust it from both sides so it will be even.

When unsaddling, remember to unhook the strap that goes between Primo's legs to the girth ring.

Good habit: When unsaddling, before taking the saddle off, pull the collar's loose end around and over the seat. Then buckle it to a ring on the near side for neat storage.

• Make sure the stirrups are adjusted correctly. The proper length for most Western riding allows one to three inches between your bottom and the saddle seat when you stand in the stirrups. Therefore, you will have to mount Primo to check the length and then dismount to make changes (or else ask someone to help you).

Stirrups vary in how they are adjusted. Some stirrup leathers have tongued buckles like belts. Others require lacing and are a big pain to adjust! Most leathers have easily adjustable holes, buckles with posts, and sliding sleeves. The posts fit into the holes and then a metal or leather sleeve slides down to hold the buckle in place.

Securing the Saddle

The ride is over. You have unfastened the girth and the breast strap.
Don't just pull the saddle off and leave the straps hanging loose.
Secure the loose ends. Here is a neatly secured barrel racing saddle,
viewed from the left side. The girth strap is wrapped. The breast
strap is laid across the saddle seat and buckled around the stirrup.
You can also hang the bridle on the horn with the reins neatly
looped.

Here's the same secured saddle viewed from the right side. Both front
and rear cinches are secured to the keeper by their buckle tongues.
The breast strap stays buckled to the D-ring on its off side, while the
rest of it goes over the seat. The saddle in both these pictures is tidy,
but the saddle pad is crooked. Be sure yours is always evenly placed.

The Bridle

Sometimes it's difficult to figure out how a piece of tack (halter, breast collar, bridle, etc.) will fit on Primo and be fastened. An easy way to work things out is first to picture how it will be worn by Primo. Then look at the buckles and the leather, and think: always put the smoothest side of the leather next to Primo; the buckles always fasten so they'll grip tighter (not pull loose) under a strain; and strap ends point down or in whichever direction best keeps them from flopping when Primo moves.

Before you start to fit the bridle on Primo, hold the bridle by the headstall crown, centered, and let the reins drop. Examine how the reins hang from the bit rings. The reins always fall *behind* the mouthpiece, so they can come back along Primo's neck into your hands. This is one way you can tell front from back. If there's a curb chain, it goes in back, too. If the headstall has a throatlatch, it'll buckle on the left side.

When you can tell the back from the front, hold the bridle so that the reins and parts that go behind Primo's chin would come off your hand first. Bend your elbow and raise your arm just high enough for the headstall to slide about midway up your arm—far enough to free your hand but not past your elbow. Also center the rein (or reins). Don't leave one side dangling or you could trip over it. After a few times, it will become an automatic way for carrying the bridle. The way it hangs on your arm is also the correct way to hang it up for storage.

• If Primo wears a halter, unbuckle it and refasten it around his neck so he'll still be tied. Primo should stand quietly for this, but if you feel he might walk away before you can

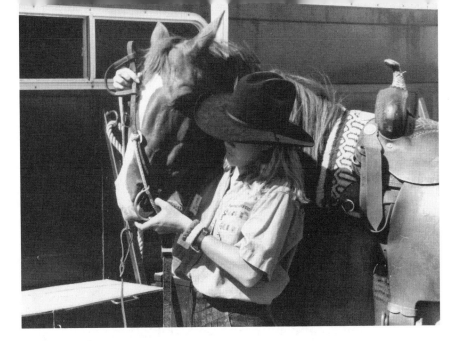

Bridling Primo

Standing at Rooster's favorite spot, Sunny bridles him with the snaffle gag used in Chapter 3. Her right hand holds the headstall while her left hand guides the bit into his mouth.

Sunny pulls the crown over both of Rooster's ears at once. Then she'll pull his right ear through the sliding ear piece. Notice how the gag bit hangs before the rein is pulled. Rooster wears a couple of deep "smile" wrinkles while the headstall gets pulled over his ears. Notice also the girth strap. The knot is finished. The end is looped up and through the keeper.

fasten the halter around his neck, slip the rein over his head to his neck, and hold him with the rein if necessary.

If Primo raises his head to resist the rein, stay calm. He may have a good reason for not wanting his ear touched. Coax him into relaxing. Sometimes it helps just to change your position. "Listen" to your horse. If he seems to tell you that he'd rather have you move more behind or in front of his head, then do it. You can actually see him relax when you find the right spot.

• Slide the headstall from your arm down into your hand. Use whichever hand is more comfortable for you. At one time or another, you'll be using both hands and most fingers. You are ready to put the bridle on Primo. It's a good idea at this time to caress Primo's nose and chin. He will enjoy this and also be aware that you now plan to work around his nose and chin.

• Supporting the headstall with one hand, grasp the bit in your other hand and gently guide it into his mouth. If you're lucky, Primo will open up and take the bit. If not, never use the bit to force his teeth apart.

To get Primo to unclench his teeth, slide a finger or thumb into the corner of his mouth, where the bit will eventually fit after he lets it in. Don't worry, Primo has no teeth at this spot, the bars of his mouth. Slide your finger in so that your first knuckle will be between his upper and lower gums, then jiggle the finger up and down to make it rock against both bars. Or press on his lower bar with your thumb. Either way, this should signal Primo to unclench his teeth and open his mouth.

• Slide the bit into place, and make sure it goes *over* his tongue. If it goes under, take the bit out and begin again.

Be very careful not to let the bit hit against Primo's teeth. It could happen as you put the bit in or as you are taking

Sunny is changing bridles. The tie-down goes on first. She adjusts the nose loop so it will lay just far enough down.

Sunny puts the bridle on. This bit is a good combination for barrel racing—a curb with loose shanks for leverage and a broken mouthpiece (like a snaffle) for lateral control.

the bridle off, particularly if Primo raises his head after you slip the headpiece over his ears. Try to keep the headstall from falling off when you remove it, and don't take the bit out until his head is low enough for you to have control of the bit's exit.

You probably will not have any trouble. Not at first, anyway. If Primo has good manners, he won't offer any resistance until perhaps after you accidentally give him reason to argue. So, take your time and do it right from the beginning.

• For a curb chain or strap, keep your free hand near Primo's mouth and hold the chain back so it can pass over his chin. If it's a tight fit to get the curb chain over Primo's chin and the bit into his mouth, unfasten the chain on its near side when you put the bridle on and take it off.

• For a noseband, use the same hand that controls the curb chain to guide the band over his nose.

Even if you go slowly and carefully, this part will probably take less time to do than to read. Once you get the bit in, you still have to get the headstall over Primo's ears. You must also hold the headstall up to keep the bit from falling out of Primo's mouth.

There are many ways to get the headstall over a horse's ears. You'll just have to experiment to see which way Primo prefers. One way, if there's enough slack in the headpiece, is for you to hold it with both hands and ease the crown over both ears at the same time, so that the ears fold backward. Some horses like this way of "getting it over with fast." Once you have the crown over Primo's ears, so there's no danger of the bit falling out, then you can ease an ear piece or browband back over to the front. Some horses might want you to do one ear at a time. Hold the crown up in front of Primo's ears, reach under it and cup an ear in your

Sunny is pulling Rooster's ear through the sliding ear piece.

Rooster's halter is strapped around his neck while he's being tacked up. Notice how it's tied to the trailer. Sunny makes the half hitch with an extra wrap-around. Then she pushes the end of the rope through the loop for extra security. If you do this, however, you first need to pull the rope's end out of the loop before you can pull on it to release the knot.

hand. Ease the ear back through so that the crown lies behind it. Do the same for the other ear. For an ear-piece headstall, it's a good idea to save the looped side for last. Then you'll already have one ear under the crown to hold the headstall in place, in case Primo becomes touchy about having his ear eased through the loop.

• The proper fit of the bit is most important. Usually, the bridle a horse comes with will already fit him properly, but this is not always so. You can determine how the bit fits in Primo's mouth once the crown is over his ears. Of course, the headstall must first be long enough to fit over his ears after the bit is in his mouth. If you can see that it's going to be too short, take the bit out of his mouth before lengthening the headstall at the cheek pieces. Then start over.

A leverage (curb) bit should make Primo's cheeks puff out slightly. A "smile" wrinkle means the bit is too tight. If his cheeks are squeezed by the cheek piece or by the shanks, the bit is too small. If he wears, say, a 5-inch bit, move up to a 5½-inch.

A snaffle bit is worn slightly tighter. A smile with one wrinkle is usually right, but two wrinkles mean that a bit is too tight.

• When the headstall is in place, check the curb chain. It should be just long enough to allow for two fingers to go between the chain and Primo's lower jaw. A chain that is too loose will pinch the corners of Primo's mouth. This is because you have to pull the rein way back before the shank can make a grip between the bit and the chain to give leverage. Although it may seem logical that the tighter the chain, the faster it will make Primo stop, it really doesn't work that way. If the chain is too tight, the shank will not have room to slide back so that the bit and chain can make a grip. You won't get any leverage when you pull the rein.

• If you have a throatlatch, fasten it. You should be able to stick four fingers under it when Primo is at rest, to allow room for the increase in his neck's size when he flexes at the poll (arches his neck).

• Finally, if Primo wears a tie-down, hook the strap to the ring on his breast collar. If he also wears draw reins, pass one split rein through each loop.

Now, Primo's tacked up and ready for you to ride!

CHAPTER 5

―◆―

Getting Up and Getting Going

Occasionally, you may have to mount or dismount Primo from his far (right) side. Almost all the time, however, you will do both from his near side. Remember: "Left is right and right is wrong."

Mounting Primo

Stand facing the saddle, but keep an eye on Primo's head for signs of what he might be thinking. Take the reins with your left hand so that you can also grab a handful of mane near the saddle with that hand. Remember: "mane and rein." If Primo's mane has been cut off (roached), hold his withers like a knob.

There are two reasons why it is better to grab Primo's mane rather than the saddle horn. First, you make contact and communicate with him. Your hold on Primo's mane and rein tells him you're about to get on his back. Primo feels your grip tighten on his mane just before you lift. That tells him your foot is in the stirrup, now here you come. Second, you are less likely to pull the saddle over if you use his mane instead of the horn for pulling yourself up. Of course, the girth should be tight enough to hold the saddle in place. But a saddle with the girth tight enough to hold, once you are up, might possibly slide while you mount. This could happen if a horse's withers are round (flat) and have little or no point. A breast collar would help keep the saddle from sliding.

Hold the reins just tight enough to make contact with Primo's bit. A mannerly horse should stand perfectly still while being mounted, but don't push your luck by leaving Primo's reins too loose. Don't pull them tight, either, or he might take this as a signal to back up as you swing into the saddle. If Primo moves, calmly but firmly tell him "Whoa." He must not move until he receives your signal to do so.

With your right hand, turn the stirrup toward you and guide your left foot in just far enough to support yourself when you put your weight on it. Whether you're mounting or riding, *your foot should never be any deeper in the stirrup than the ball of your foot.* A foot that's wedged in too far can get caught. If you should fall off, you'll get dragged.

You have "mane and rein" in your left hand and your left foot is in the stirrup. What's next?

Pull on the saddle, either the cantle or the horn, with your right hand and spring up off your right foot. (Don't jab Primo's side with your left toe as you lift off!) When you've lifted yourself high enough, lean forward over him. Arch your back just enough to center your weight over his back and swing your right leg over. If you use the horn, your pull will help swing you into the seat. If you use the cantle, move your hand for your leg to pass over.

After you get your right leg across, use your knees to control your body's weight, and lower yourself as gently and gracefully as possible into the saddle. Never ever just plop yourself onto Primo's back! This hurts his back. Primo won't want to stand quietly for you to mount after you've "crash-landed" a few times.

Slip your right foot in the stirrup, make sure you have the reins even (not hanging loose on one side), then straighten up so that you sit tall in the saddle. Before you do anything else, take a deep breath. Let it out slowly and then *smile*! A big smile helps you to relax, which in turn relaxes Primo.

Mounting Primo

There's no point in saying exactly where to stand to mount because a lot depends on your size and Primo's. Sunny has found her spot. She's put her foot in the stirrup, grabbed a handful of mane, rein and the cantle, and is ready to lift off. Rooster's ears and eye show that he's expecting her.

Balanced nicely, and without poking Rooster's side with her toe, up and over she goes. Sunny's reins have just enough slack for control if she needs it, and so does the tie-down. She should have been looking over Rooster's ears, however, instead of at the trailer. For a step-off dismount, simply reverse the procedures shown here and in the next picture.

What do you do if, when you try to straighten up, you find that the saddle has slipped to the left?

Stand in the stirrups, take some weight off your left foot and shift it to your right foot by pushing down in the right stirrup. If the saddle slides too far or too fast to the right, the girth is too loose and will need tightening.

Sometimes you need to leave Primo saddled a while before you ride him. Do him a favor, meanwhile, and loosen his girth. Remember to tighten it, of course, before you ride again.

Assistance in Mounting

Primo may be a pony or he may be a full-size horse. If you cannot reach over Primo's withers and at least touch his opposite shoulder from the ground, you may have difficulty mounting.

One way to deal with this problem is to use a mounting block. It can be anything that's high enough and sturdy enough not to tip over when you push off to swing up and over. A stool, a bench, a hay bale or a tree stump are all fine. Lead Primo close enough to the block for you to reach him from it, but not too close. Otherwise, he could knock the block over or get tangled in it, which might make him panic.

Sometimes, it's better to have someone help you mount. That person should stand to the left of you so he won't get in the way when you swing on and also in case he needs to help hold Primo.

In keeping Primo still and giving you a boost, your helper holds the rein or tie-down strap with his left hand. He cups his right hand for you to step into like a stirrup. Meanwhile, you hold mane, rein and saddle. Do a good job of pulling with your hands as you mount, so you won't need Superman to help. Once you're up, put your feet in the stirrups.

Or, your helper can brace his left leg for extra support, then bend *his* right knee for you to step on his right thigh. Use it like a mounting block.

If you don't need your helper to hold Primo steady, he can use both hands and lace his fingers together for a "living stirrup." By keeping his own knees flexible, he should have no difficulty lifting you into the saddle. But you must help by pulling. This is how one little kid can help another little kid mount a not-so-little horse.

Assisted Mount
Cyrus uses my "living stirrup" (the fingers of both hands laced together) to climb on Bo. Although Cyrus has mane and rein, I also have Bo's left rein tucked under my arm.

Dismounting

Here is the most common Western way to dismount:

1. Keep your reins in contact with Primo's mouth and slip your foot out of the far stirrup. The reins should be just tight enough for you to have control of him until both of your feet are on the ground. If your rein hand is your right hand, switch the reins to your left hand.
2. Keep your head level and look at Primo's head while you lean slightly forward, holding some part of the pommel lightly to balance yourself. Arch your back just enough to keep your shoulders straight, like when you're riding, and swing your right leg over Primo's back.

3. After your leg has passed over, grasp the cantle with your right hand. Keep your left foot in the stirrup and *gracefully* step down.

4. After your right foot is on the ground, hold some part of the saddle with your left hand for balance. Then smoothly let your left foot down. If it's a big reach to the ground, where you can't just back out your left foot, you run the risk of getting it hung in the stirrup. Stand on tiptoe with your right foot and with your right hand, ease your left foot out of the stirrup.

Rather than step down, you may prefer to *vault* down. This is more common in English riding, but you can also do it Western style:

1. Do everything as explained in steps 1 through 3, up to the point of keeping your left foot in the stirrup and stepping down.

2. Just as you straighten up, place more weight on your hands (lean across at your hips, too, if this makes you feel more secure) so you can slip your left foot out of the stirrup.

3. Now, drop down and land on both feet. Keep one or both hands in contact with the saddle or with Primo and with the reins as you slide. Don't worry, your hands will instinctively find the best places to make contact. This contact keeps you lined up in a good position to control Primo and yourself.

Falling or Getting Thrown Off

Any horseman will tell you, "If you've never fallen off a horse, you haven't done much riding." A Western saddle gives you more protection against falling off than an English saddle or riding bareback. But sooner or later, you and Primo are bound to part company. In case it happens sooner rather than later, now is a good time to learn how to fall off correctly. Practice the methods in a small, enclosed area that has soft ground. Wear a hard hat and have a helper with you.

Here are several possible ways for you to suddenly part company with Primo, with some pointers for safer landings:

1. If you're suddenly *thrown* off, one way to land is on your hands. Don't keep your arms stiff. "Curl in" and fold on impact. This helps guard against a sprain or break. Roll out of Primo's way so you won't get kicked or rolled on (which can happen if he also falls).
2. If you're going off backward, try to twist or roll over so you won't land flat on your back. Again, roll out of Primo's way. If you are falling off backward, it could be because he reared. He could fall over backward, too.
3. If your head or shoulder is aimed to hit the ground first, tuck your head to save your neck. This could happen if, say, you fell while Primo did a quick pivot. Place both hands behind your neck, drop your chin, tuck in your elbows and shoulder blades. Land behind your shoulder, then roll.

In these three situations, don't worry about the reins or controlling Primo. Concentrate on protecting yourself. Think about making a ball of yourself and rolling to get out of Primo's way as soon as you hit the ground. Then you'll probably do everything right instinctively.

It's a good idea to learn to do a shoulder roll. Do it on a tumbling mat, not Primo! Also, most horses will avoid stepping on you because by nature a horse sees you as "unsafe footing." You are too soft for him.

Now that we've talked about the scary ways of landing, let's talk about landing on your feet. It's the safest way and almost as easy as vaulting off for a regular dismount.

Bailing Out

Many times, you'll know when you have lost your balance and are about to fall. You'll also know which side you're about to go off. If it's too late to recover your balance, you still can control your fall by "bailing out" (doing an emergency dismount).

This is what you do:

1. Lean forward and hold on to something in addition to the reins while you take both feet out of the stirrups. It's better to grab Primo's mane ("mane and rein") instead of the horn because your sudden weight shift can pull a loose saddle over to one side and panic your horse. The most important thing to remember, once you know you're going off, is to *slide or kick both feet out of the stirrups*.

2. For going off to the left, bring your right leg over Primo's back, and then vault off. This is like a regular vaulting dismount, except that you must push off stronger with both hands in front. Then arch your back more to raise your right leg so it can clear the cantle. Your right hand can be anywhere on the seat but not on the cantle. Your right leg will be easier to control if you straighten your knee and point your toes as you do when you dive.

3. Push against Primo with your left hand as you go off. This gets your legs clear of his body and saddle, so your feet can drop freely to the ground.

4. Keep your right hand or arm in contact with Primo's body or the saddle. This hug keeps you from going too far away from Primo after pushing and will also slow your slide.

5. Slide down Primo's shoulder and land on your feet with your body turned so you're ready to run alongside. Bend your knees to absorb the shock of landing.

6. Take a step or two forward to keep up with Primo. At first you may need to run, although he'll probably slow down and stop as soon as he feels you go off. Try to

Bailing Out

Sunny has lost her balance and feels that she's falling off to the left. She slips both feet out of the stirrups, leans forward and grabs Rooster's mane as well as the rein. Note her *safety helmet*.

keep your hold on the rein and keep contact with Primo's mane, neck and shoulder or the saddle. Should you drop the rein or reins and Primo gets ahead of you, never grab for his tail. Accidentally or instinctively, he might kick you.

When you bail out on the right side, follow the same directions but do everything "right" instead of "left."

Practice bailing out first from a standstill and practice from each side. Then, *after* you learn to ride Primo at a walk, trot and lope, and feel that you have control, try bailing out at these gaits. If you practice too much, Primo will start anticipating your moves. He'll stop every time you lean forward and shift your weight like you do for vaulting off.

She supports her weight on both hands and swings her right leg over Rooster's back for a vaulting "bail out" dismount.

She pushes off for control as she slides down.

She keeps contact after she lands, for control.

Still holding the reins and keeping contact with Rooster, Sunny takes a couple of quick steps to keep up with him until she can stop him.

A Realistic View of Western Riding

Do not ride Primo the way you see horses ridden in Westerns. Some actors really are fine horsemen, but most movie and TV "cowboys" don't know how to ride well. Look at how often they grab leather! Also, movies use lots of dust and motion to keep up the excitement. For example, a horse gallops hard, comes to a bouncy stop, then gets jerked around to gallop back up the same road.

Things don't happen that way in the real world of Western riding. Watch a good rider take a horse through a smooth rollback. A rollback uses a stop, a reverse and a change of lead at a full gallop. It follows the same pattern taken by the movie horse, but what a difference in how it's done! This and other trained moves at high speed, including barrel racing, are beautiful and exciting to watch, and a thrill to ride.

Most Western riding, however, is done at a relaxed pace and in a relaxed manner. The goal in Western riding is for the horse to do almost everything on his own and for the person on his back to be along just for the ride. There's really a lot more going on between horse and rider, but it's supposed to *look* like the rider is just sitting there. The rider is also supposed to look like he or she is part of the horse. For this really to be so, the rider must work in perfect harmony with the horse. You're off to a good start by "thinking like a horse" for what you've done so far.

Seat and Balance

Riding in perfect harmony requires your good seat and balance. You can find good seat and balance on Primo much easier if you first learn about the differences in bone structure between girls and boys and the center of balance (CB for short). Read everything here about structural differences. Don't skip parts that you think won't apply to you because you're a boy or you're a girl. Some important facts for everyone are mixed in with matters that apply mainly to girls or to boys, because the facts make more sense if you can see right away how they relate to structural differences in our bodies.

There are three kinds of seat: (1) the *normal* or basic seat for most riding; (2) the *forward* seat to move your weight forward when Primo moves *his* weight forward; and (3) the *deep* seat to give you increased seatbone control.

The Normal Seat

The basic normal seat balances you naturally on Primo's back so that he also feels comfortable and moves willingly. After you mount, stand in the stirrups and let your heels drop down, then lower yourself until your crotch barely touches the saddle. Before putting your full weight on the saddle, adjust your pelvis so that, when you do settle, your weight is evenly divided between your buttocks and your crotch. You are *on* rather than *in* the saddle, with your ears, shoulders, hips and heels in line. Think of your weight as flowing

Normal Seat
Teresa has a nice normal seat on Gold Alibi, nicknamed Pal, but her stirrups should be longer. (Look at Sunny's stirrups. They're just right.) Teresa shows English style as well as Western style. The stirrups are supposed to be shorter for hunter seat. After she saw these pictures, Teresa lowered her stock-seat stirrups and assumed a sensational Western seat!

down into your heels. Your feet, knees and hip joints absorb most of Primo's movements. A good normal seat lets you relax, but you still need good posture and balance.

The Forward Seat

For the forward seat, you'll carry more weight on the front edges of your seatbones *and* on the insides of your thighs for a three-point (bottom plus legs) position. But your bottom doesn't touch the saddle for a two-point position. You'll only

Forward Seat
Teresa rolls up to demonstrate a good forward seat. Teresa's show saddle is very handsome, with its laced oxbow stirrups.

use your legs to straddle. Your upper body moves more with Primo's motion. The forward seat needs more than good balance. You also have to use more leg muscles to keep your knees (really the thigh area just above your knees) against the saddle to act as shock absorbers. Your ankles will act as shock absorbers, too. After Primo finishes galloping or doing whatever else shifts his weight and CB forward, return to a normal seat.

Deep Seat
Teresa tucks and drives her seatbones for a deep seat. This is also a good example of a "cutter's slouch."

The Deep Seat

The deep seat enables you to communicate with Primo when you want to do lateral moves and other fine-tune work. You'll sit up straight and flex the muscles deep in your abdomen. (The next section will explain this in detail.) Your seatbones are pushed down so that they can "talk" and "listen" to Primo.

Differences in Bone Structure

Boys and girls have different bone structures and this causes boys and girls to function differently in the saddle. The main difference is in the pelvis, then in the lower back and thighs. These differences in turn cause other differences in the knees and ankles.

We must also consider other important factors. Boys have bones that make it easier for them to sit correctly in the saddle. Girls' bodies are more flexible and sensitive. Girls can feel Primo's changes sooner. Boys and girls each have a chance to be "best" at something. All in all, we're pretty equally matched for riding horses.

A boy is built so that his pelvis "wants" to sit squarely. He can easily rock backward onto his tailbone and use it like a stool. Girls balance more comfortably by rolling the pelvis slightly forward. Until taught how to control certain muscles, it's natural for girls to sit swaybacked.

It's easier for a boy to be a good natural rider, especially Western style. He relaxes sooner and seems very comfortable because he discovers how to roll back onto his "stool" and "sit on his hip pockets." For most guys, this is a normal seat. Many men ride for years using this seat, thinking they have a "deep, relaxed seat." But it's really only a slouch.

Differences in the Pelvis

The drawings in the top row are right-side views of a girl's pelvis and the drawings in the middle row are of a boy's pelvis, also in the three seat positions. The horizontal broken lines represent Primo's back. The pelvises differ in (1) the angle and shape of the tailbones (the girl's is shorter and tilts back, the boy's curves under); (2) where the tailbone and lower back vertebrae appear within the pelvic area, shown by a curved broken line representing the pelvis; (3) where the hip bones "divide" the seatbones, shown in the bottom row; and (4) the tilt of the pelvis.

Drawings 1 and 4 show the girl and boy in a forward seat. The girl has her pelvis in a good position. However, she forgot to use her posture muscles to straighten her lower "building blocks." There is too much curve between her bottom vertebra and her tailbone. It's weak. She sits swaybacked.

Drawings 2 and 5 show them both in a normal seat. The boy's body weight makes his bottom vertebrae a bit lower than the girl's, but they both have a good normal seat.

Drawings 3 and 6 show them in a deep seat. They've dropped their seatbone "stingers" to check or stop the horse. Both are at a good angle on their seatbones. You can see how the girl has dropped her seatbones by comparing where her hip bone divides her pelvis here with the drawing of her normal seat. The boy is heavier and is seated deep enough for his second vertebra to dip below the tip of the pelvis. The girl hasn't dropped below her first vertebra.

Drawings 7 and 8 show the pelvis as it contacts the saddle. The crotch is at the top and the tailbone is at the bottom center. The hip socket and the seatbones are black so you can identify them easier. The broken line represents the axis, or the center of balance, bottom view. The girl's pelvis is on the left. Her axis crosses the middle of her hip sockets and the front of her seatbones. This is why the forward seat is more natural for her. The boy's axis crosses the middle of his seatbones and the front of his hip sockets. This is why the normal seat is more natural for him. The girl's pelvis is wider than the boy's pelvis. Her seatbones fan out at wider angles, too.

Good riders do not slouch. A "cutter's slouch," however, is not a slouch. It's a special Western version of a good deep seat. It gets the rider's weight off the horse's front end and lets the rider stay with the horse while performing extremely fast changes of direction.

A boy's slouch comes from down low. A girl slouches from higher up. Sometimes it starts about midback, but usually it happens right around the shoulder blades. Most girls slouch by rounding their shoulders.

How is a boy cured of slouching?

He learns to shift his weight more to the front of his seatbones. He will lower his crotch by tilting or pushing it down to the saddle.

A boy's lower back is nearly straight up and down, but a girl's lower back is naturally curved. A girl's body is better suited to the forward seat than to the normal seat. For a girl to stop slouching, she just has to straighten her shoulders. If a girl is told to place her weight more to the front of her seatbones and lower her crotch by pushing it down to the saddle, she'll likely respond by swaying or hollowing her back even more. Not only does this look just as bad as slouching, it's also very uncomfortable and can damage her back.

In both boys and girls, good posture happens by arranging the vertebrae (backbones) into a comfortable but relatively straight line from the pelvis and tailbone up through the neck.

It's like stacking blocks. Riding a horse really works those little blocks, so you must line them all up correctly.

In fact, good riding is impossible without good posture. In order to follow Primo's motion, your lower back has to be limber enough to move freely back and forth and side to side. If one block moves out of place, or if the muscles affected by the blocks keep getting pushed or pulled from the wrong angle, this will cause you to stiffen up somewhere. This sets up a chain reaction that affects your riding and, unless corrected, also gives Primo bad habits because you're actually giving him bad commands.

How can girls overcome their natural swaybacks and line up the blocks to sit in a three-point position?

Girls must develop and fine-tune their lower abdominal muscles, especially the key posture muscle, the iliopsoas (ill-e-o-SO-us), which spreads out in the abdomen to cover most of the pelvis and tailbone. Girls must tuck their buttocks under *without* changing leg pressure. Boys have the same muscles and can use them in similar ways, but usually don't have to think about them. Their bones naturally let them do what girls have to work harder at doing.

Improving Your Posture

To find your posture muscles and experiment with them, you might want to try these exercises at home. First, lie on your back on a mat or cloth or on your bed and spread your legs about as wide as they'd be if you were seated on Primo. Place your hands slightly away from your sides, palms down, and then relax completely.

- Imagine that someone is about to hit your lower abdomen. Tighten the muscles in your abdomen to protect yourself. At the same time, keep your belly and chest areas as relaxed as possible. *Breathe from your belly*, not from the top of your lungs. Proper breathing is very important for both girls and boys, especially when active.
- As you flex the muscles in your lower abdomen, tuck

your "tail" as you would for protection against a spanking.

- After you've experimented lying down, stand up and try the same tighten/tuck exercise. As you tuck your buttocks, you'll naturally want to bend your knees slightly. You may even feel your heels "want" to lower. Flexed correctly, these posture muscles can straighten a girl's lower back and make her pelvis tuck under, without her having to hold her breath or become tense.

Since muscles (like bones) all "tie together" somewhere along the line, the posture muscles need cooperation from certain leg muscles and ligaments that attach to the hip, knee and ankle joints.

Each individual rider needs to experiment to find out how those muscles work together. Girls especially should experiment and try these exercises:

- At home, lie down on your back with your knees bent and your feet a few inches away from a wall. Raise your legs and, with your knees bent slightly as if your feet were in the stirrups, rest your feet against the wall. Shift most of your weight to your upper back, so that your pelvic area is free to move and rotate. In other words, you're ready to "walk up the wall." Now, combine the abdominal muscle experiments with the leg aid experiments described in Chapter 2.
- Practice pushing your feet different ways against the wall "stirrups" to move your seatbones (each and both).
- Practice flexing to tuck your tail.
- Stay on your back and "walk" away from the wall. (Doing this by itself is a good exercise for flexing your

back.) Flex the front, mid and back parts of your calves and thighs, plus knee area.

You can flex the front of your calf by pushing down and pointing with your big toe. This will cause your heel to raise, but don't worry about that now. You're working on being limber, not on proper stirrup position. Flex the mid part of your calf by rolling your ankle. Flex the back of your calf by dropping your heel.

It's better for you to figure out on your own how to flex different parts of your thigh than it is for me to tell you exactly how to do it. What works for me might not work for you, and vice versa. I will tell you this, however. You'll need to move muscles in your abdomen and in your buttocks. You'll shift your seatbones, hips and knees, too.

As you experiment on one area, you'll discover more and more ways to control it and make it tie in with other areas. Before we move on down from posture muscles, remember this: keep your pelvis "loose." Your pelvis should be able to rotate freely in all directions.

After you've learned the chain reaction of your leg, back and abdominal muscles, then you need to practice stretching your leg muscles. They have to loosen and work on their own, independent of what your posture muscles do, because that is the key to getting your blocks lined up.

Boys also have to stretch some leg muscles, particularly the tendons that raise and lower the heel. A boy's ankles tend to be stiffer than a girl's. I realized this when, as a swim coach, I taught the breaststroke. Boys had more trouble turning out their ankles and loosening them for doing the kick.

Work on stretching those tendons until your heels fall into place easily when you put your feet in the stirrups. A good exercise is to sit or lie down and rotate your ankles by pointing your toes and "drawing" circles in the air. The bigger and rounder and more to the outside you can make your circles, the more flexible your ankles will be. This is also a good way to loosen ankles that become stiff from being in the stirrup too long. Just slip your foot out of the stirrup and draw circles with it.

Back to bones, usually a boy's knee is attached squarely onto his thighbone, but a girl's knee is offset. This makes a boy's knees "look" straight ahead and a girl's knees "look" toward each other. Riding without stirrups, a boy's feet usually hang nearly level, while a girl's relaxed feet point more downward and inward. Even though a girl might start out with her heels more raised than a boy's, her ability to be more flexible makes it easier for her to drop her heels down to the proper position for using stirrups.

Its easier for a boy to sit smoothly when Primo jogs (or even trots faster) and lopes than for most girls. The reason is the angle of the hip. It's easier for a boy to rest the inner surface of his thighs flat against the saddle, to keep his knees close to the saddle without squeezing, and to point his toes forward.

Girls make up for this bone difference by their special ability to control the abdominal muscles. They use these muscles (and the muscles in their thighs) to relax and thereby open, or widen, the angle of the hip joints.

To get an idea of what I mean, think of a pair of pliers. It can pick up a pin when the joint is at one end of the slot. It can also pick up a much wider object, but only after you slide the nut to the opposite end of the slot. It's pretty much the same with the hip joints. A girl can "pick up" a deeper seat on Primo by sliding her hip joints so that her thighbones open wider. The better a girl becomes at sliding her hip joints (without letting her back or leg muscles get stiff), the easier it is for her to keep her knees at a wider angle, so they face each other less and "look" more straight ahead.

Differences in the Feet and Legs

Sitting double on Bo, Cyrus and Erin show how, without stirrups, a boy's feet hang differently from a girl's. Generally, a boy's feet will be nearly level with the ground. Notice how his knees point more forward than Erin's. Both Cyrus and Erin are lined up nicely on Bo's back (except Erin has her chin on Cyrus's shoulder). Look at this picture again after you look at the next picture. Cyrus's stirrups are too short. Erin's legs bend about the same, with or without stirrups. We see some differences, but each rider has a good seat for his/her build and the size of his/her horse.

Sitting Up Straight

Good seat is based on how you contact Primo's back. If you imagined yourself "sitting up straight," you might picture being *pushed* straight upward from your lower backbones.

What about how the rest of you, above your waist? If you sit like a rod is stuck up your back, you'll be more than straight, you'll be stiff. What happens when Primo moves? Your body from the waist down needs to be flexible to move with him. But you don't want the rest of you, from your waist up, to be so loose that you flop around when you ride.

Let's look at the problem of sitting up straight, starting from the top. Imagine a string coming out of the top of your head. Now imagine a great hand in the sky gently lifting you up by that string, like you're a puppet. The hand is very skillful. It pulls you just enough to line up your blocks. It doesn't lift you enough for your seat or legs to be changed. They're already lined up. The string is attached far enough back so that when it's pulled, your chin levels off. When you're pulled up tall in the saddle, you're straight, but you feel relaxed on Primo's back. You're strong and flexible, yet soft. You're not stiff or rigid.

A good rider follows many of the same posture rules as a good dancer. Keep your head, body and shoulders level. Look right over Primo's ears (except when you're planning to turn). Don't twist your body or shoulders except to counterbalance Primo's fancy moves. If your blocks line up properly, everything from your pelvis on down will be flexible and will be able to follow Primo's movements smoothly.

To picture how your legs should look when you're on Primo and viewed from the side, think of a straight line drawn from your ear to the ground. That line also crosses your shoulder, hipbone and heel. Of course, this is while

Riders' Positions

The fence emphasizes both riders' positions, although the pads in
Erin's shirt make it hard to see her shoulders. Even so, you can
envision a line drawn down through her ear, shoulder, hip and heel.
Erin has a good normal seat on big C.J., who is walking. In the
background, Cyrus drives with his seatbones to keep Bo in a lope.
His shoulders are a bit crooked and his heel is raised, but he's nicely
relaxed and in control. Both riders hold the split reins Texas style.

Primo is standing still or moving in a collected way. (We
say Primo is "collected" when he brings his back legs under
his body with each step and generally looks like he has lots
of energy very much under control.) Viewed from behind,
you are level and your legs fall relaxed against Primo's sides.
Your heels and arms are down and your toes are forward.

Center of Balance

Thanks to a natural fear of falling over backward, new riders
seldom make the mistake of leaning too far back. In fact,
they'll probably start out by leaning too far forward. They

might even try to hang on by wrapping their legs back in a death grip with toes pointing toward Primo's hind feet. In these positions the horse and rider are not in balance or moving in harmony.

Your center of balance (CB for short) is located somewhere behind your belly button. Regardless of how long Primo's body is, his center of balance is directly under where you sit to be most comfortable and secure. This makes it handy for matching your CB with Primo's.

Keeping in Balance with Primo

There is no substitute for the many hours you'll spend riding to learn the feel of moving in harmony with Primo. He'll wear a bridle for those rides. The following experiments *without* a bridle (or with the reins looped over your saddle horn) can help you understand balance by feeling Primo move in unexpected yet safe ways. They'll also prove how much you depend upon your vision for keeping balance. Find an enclosed area where you can practice. You'll need a helper to lead Primo. And you *should* wear a safety helmet.

Close your eyes and don't hold on to anything while the helper leads Primo around. What did you feel?

If Primo is walking in a straight line, you should feel regular front-back rocks of your pelvis and side-to-side shifts of your seatbones. Your bones are being moved as your body automatically follows the motion in Primo's body each time he lifts his back leg.

If Primo stumbles, turns, stops suddenly or changes gait, you'll find yourself suddenly playing catch-up. You'll probably grab leather. That's because consistency feels good, while changes are disturbing. You feel like your stack of blocks is about to tumble. Why is this?

It's because there's more to keeping harmony than knowing where the center of balance is for each of you. Let's experiment to find the missing ingredient.

While Primo walks straight and makes a few turns, roll your head front to back, then side to side. Keep your neck really limber, so your head just wobbles around, and keep your eyes closed. You'll find that the position of your head influences your balance. You have to work hard at keeping your balance when your head rolls loosely to another position, and you'll have to recover your balance if Primo makes a sudden change of any kind. This experiment proves how important a level head is for keeping your balance while riding.

For the following experiment, you'll keep your eyes open. As you continue to ride Primo, shift your weight from side to side. Then lean backward and forward. Next, twist your hips and shoulders.

Primo probably turned slightly, or at least shifted his feet when you went from side to side. He slowed when you leaned back and he wanted to go a little faster when you leaned forward. He did some more shifting when you twisted.

Was Primo reacting to your shift in center of balance? No, because you stayed on him and didn't fall off. Therefore, even though you moved, your CB stayed over his CB.

What Primo reacted to was your shift in weight. Your CB didn't shift from his CB during those exercises, but your weight did. That's the missing ingredient: weight. *Your weight has to team up with your center of balance* in order for you to ride a horse. You already do this automatically by now because you've learned that if you don't, you'll fall.

This experiment also proves that you're not the only one who has to keep making changes to adjust CB and weight.

You do it to balance *yourself* while on a moving horse, and Primo does it to balance *himself* while you're on his back. If you sway or wobble, Primo is thrown out of balance.

These experiments let you see and feel the CB/weight relationship between you and Primo at slower gaits. At this speed, you can usually move your back or seatbones enough to adjust your CB/weight and keep up with Primo's CB/weight changes without having to grab leather.

Now think about when you'll be riding faster. Maybe not a gallop, but fast enough for Primo to have some real energy in his motion (called momentum). When Primo makes a sudden change with momentum, you'll experience "weight in motion." If you don't react with your changes at the same speed that Primo changes, you'll lose your balance.

Do you remember the main reason for using a tie-down? It helps a performance horse stay out of trouble while he's working hard at doing a good job. It controls how much he uses his head as a counterbalance. For every force there must be a counterforce. For example, if Primo moves quickly to the right, you should push hard on your right stirrup. This shifts more of your own weight over to your left in order to keep your CB over Primo's. If you don't shift your weight immediately to counterbalance Primo's change, you'll probably fall off.

These experiments show how much you depend on your vision for balance. You should also use your vision to guide Primo. Always look ahead. Watch where you're going. This helps line everything up for telling Primo where to go.

How Reins Are Used

Horses ridden Western style usually are guided by both reins carried in one hand. This is called neck reining. If Primo neck-reins, you might think that's the only reining method you use. Actually you use more than one. Sometimes you use more than one at the same time. In order to tell Primo exactly what you want, you need to understand how each method works.

A *neck rein* is also called a "bearing rein." It's the classic Western way to turn a horse while riding one-handed. You hold the reins over Primo's neck and move your hand so that one rein is laid against one side of Primo's neck. Primo responds by turning in the other direction. For example, you lay the rein against the left side of his neck and he'll turn to the right.

For a *direct rein*, the pulled rein on either side works directly from mouth to rear. In two-handed riding, you pull either rein directly back to turn Primo. You pull the right rein to turn him right and the left rein to turn him left. This is done mainly for English riding, but a direct rein is also used this way for Western. Most of the time, though, you'll ride one-handed and pull back (or back and up) evenly with both reins to slow or stop Primo, or to back him. The main thing to remember is that a direct rein is pulled directly back. It's not pulled out to the side.

A *leading rein* is also called an opening rein or a plow rein. You ride two-handed to use it. It's similar to direct reining in that the rein is pulled from either side of Primo's neck. The difference is that a leading rein is pulled *out* to the side. For example, you "lead" Primo to the left by holding the left rein several inches away from his neck and pulling it. The rein "opens" the door on the left for Primo to move through. Actually "open" refers to opening the angle between the rein and Primo's neck. But an opened door paints a better picture. (It's called a plow rein because it's the way you'd ask Primo to turn if he were pulling a plow.)

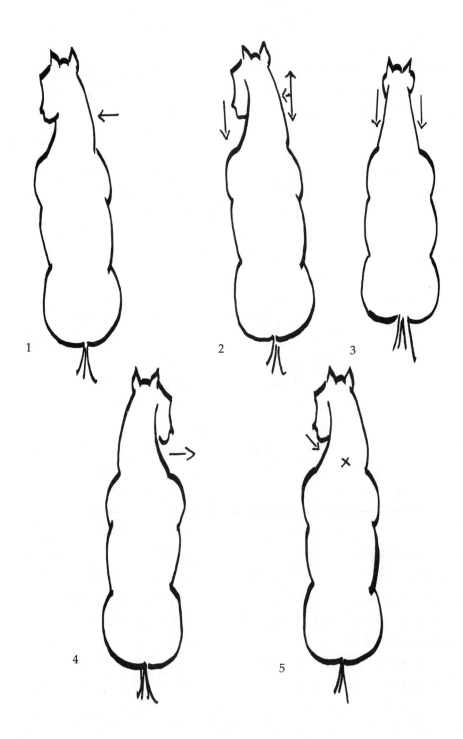

Ways to Use the Reins
1. Neck rein applied to the right side for a left turn.
2. Direct rein applied to the left side for a left turn and indirect rein applied to the right side for support.
3. Direct rein applied to both sides, to stop or check.
4. Leading rein applied to the right side for a right move.
5. Pulley rein applied to both sides for an emergency stop.

Much of Primo's training used the leading rein, and you may use it later for asking him to do certain moves.

An *indirect rein* is applied somewhat like neck reining. You put the rein against Primo's neck, or sometimes against his shoulder. The main difference is, an indirect rein is never used alone. It controls Primo's other side, not his leading side. Riding two-handed, you can use an indirect rein on one side to make corrections while the rein on the other side gives him your main cue. You use it to ask Primo to shift his weight from one side to the other (for making perfect circles or turns) or as a reminder not to drift away from, or too close to, the rail.

A *pulley rein* is an emergency brake. You grab one rein up short and press that hand hard against Primo's neck. At the same time, you really pull back and up with the other rein. Another version is the crossover. With it, you cross both reins into a strong "seesaw" against a runaway's neck.

How to Hold the Reins

For neck reining, there are two ways to hold the reins: split rein (a Texas style) and romal (a California style).

Most riders use the *split rein grip*. To use it simply lay the reins in your palm and close on them with your thumb and forefinger. You may put your index finger between the reins

Standard (Texas-style) Grip

Teresa holds the split reins in a standard grip. There's a straight line from her arm through her wrist and hand on through the reins, with plenty of slack. Her hands are nicely quiet, but too low for a Texas grip. Notice how she holds her rein hand palm down and has her free hand in front for carrying the bight. The angle of your palm doesn't matter, but your wrist should be softly straight. You may rest your free hand on your thigh or balance it forward. Both Teresa and Pal are outfitted very nicely.

A close-up of a good standard rein grip, other hand on thigh.

Romal Grip
Here are romal reins gripped properly, viewed from the off side so that you can also see how the romal is carried. (Photograph courtesy of *California Horse Review*.)

for better control. The rein slack (bight) falls from the back of your hand to either side.

In the *romal grip*, your hand holds the reins in a relaxed fist so that the reins come from the underside and out the top by your thumb. In other words, it's the opposite of the split rein grip. Another difference is that the rule books say *"no* finger between the reins" for showing a romal grip. The romal strap is carried in your other hand.

For either style, keep your wrist relatively straight. When at attention, there should be a straight line from your elbow to the rein. Your rein hand goes more or less over the horn when you're standing or going straight. Find the spot that feels most natural for you to be balanced, so your shoulder and arm can relax. Keep your other arm and hand in a position that matches your rein arm and hand, with your free hand making a relaxed fist. Or, you can rest your free hand lightly and in a relaxed manner on your thigh. You may use either hand for your rein hand, but you must stay with it and not change hands during competition. Rules for Western classes (except speed performances) do not allow your free hand to be placed on the saddle for support. Whether you plan to compete or not, better learn by the rules and form good riding habits.

For two-handed reining with a snaffle bit or hackamore, hold the rein on each side of Primo's neck. The reins pass through your hands back-to-front, romal style, except you'll probably use split reins. If you intend to show Primo in a snaffle or hackamore, you'll need to learn how to hold both reins crossed correctly. This is explained in the rule books.

Western riding is done with a looser rein than English

Two-handed Grip
A close-up of my hands using a two-handed grip.

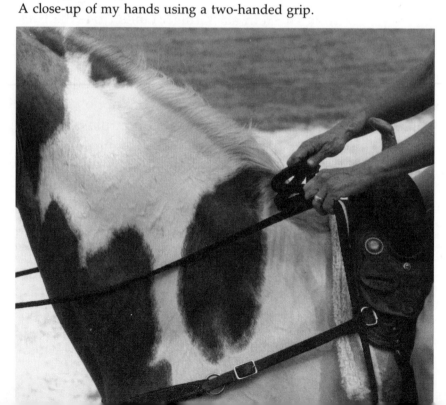

riding. This is especially true with split reins. But "loose" does not mean "hanging down"! You must at all times have rein contact with Primo in order to control him. How much contact depends on circumstances, primarily Primo's gait and speed.

You won't always hold the reins at the same spot. As Primo's neck and head change position, you'll usually move your hands to follow his motion. But sometimes you must change the rein length. To lengthen the reins, loosen your grip and let Primo pull the reins through your hand until they are long enough, then tighten your grip to stop the reins' slide. More often, the reins need to be shortened. To do this one-handed, simply loosen the grip on your rein hand and pull out the slack behind it with your free hand. For taking up slack two-handed, do the same thing, one rein at a time, using the other hand. Or, you can move each rein through your hand and take up slack by bending your fingers and pushing with your thumb.

Before you finally use a bridle on Primo, you might want to try this experiment so you'll know what Primo feels when you pull the rein. You'll need a partner and a bridle. Although Primo probably uses a curb, the experiment will work better if you use a snaffle bit. You can't really feel what a curb bit does.

Have your partner grip the headstall crown with one hand and the bit with the other hand. Face your partner and hold one rein in each hand, as for two-handed reining. Use direct reins to cue right and left turns, just like you would ask Primo. Use leading reins to signal right and left turns. Use two direct reins to ask for a stop. As you do all this, *watch* the reins move the mouthpiece.

Now trade places with your partner and *feel* the mouthpiece move while he or she moves the reins, doing the same things you did. Think to yourself, This is what Primo feels. Adjust your grip on the bit to imitate Primo with a "soft" mouth (relaxed grip) and a "hard" mouth (tighter grip). Have your partner repeat the rein routines while you hold the bit using these two grips. As you feel each change from the bit's end, again think, This is what Primo feels.

This experiment gives you a feel for Primo's reins. It also helps you develop good hands.

Mistakes made with improper use of the reins outnumber all other mistakes made by beginning riders. For example, a timid rider will leave too much slack in the reins and lose control. Another rider will hold the reins too tight and hurt the horse's mouth. Usually, however, a beginner will lose patience because the horse doesn't obey what the rider *thinks* instead of what he or she *signals*. Use think-talk, but don't ask Primo to read your mind. *Keep your hand, leg and body (weight) signals clear.*

Seeing Things from Primo's Point of View

People (including trainers) and horses differ in more ways than meet the eye. They have different personalities and see things from different points of view. Because of these differences, there's more than one way to get a horse to do almost anything.

Before he's trained, a horse will usually push against steady pressure and give in to sudden or short-term pressure. That's his instinct. He'll also instinctively move himself under his rider's weight in order to keep his own balance. Primo will try to keep exactly underneath you.

Western horses are trained to move *away* from even the lightest pressure, particularly from the reins. Some continue to lean into pressure, however, to use it like a crutch even after they're trained.

Your success as a rider depends on your ability to find and use whichever signals work best with any horse you ride. I'll explain the basic ways to give your signal.

The rest is up to you.

Getting Primo to Go

To begin walking, squeeze slightly with your calves or buttocks and relax the reins a little by moving your hands an inch or two forward. This should signal Primo to move. He should move straight forward and not start off by turning. If Primo doesn't move, lift the reins so he'll feel contact through the bit. Nudge him with your heel, and make a clicking or kissing sound. Do these sound cues softly. Otherwise, Primo might misunderstand and start off too fast.

Better yet, use think-talk. "Unnecessary talking" gets you marked down in most classes if you compete. Besides, it's fun to be in secret mental harmony with your horse.

As Primo moves along, keep enough contact with the rein to feel the rhythmic bobbing of his head. Use what you learned from your bridle-holding experiment to develop good hands. "Give in" to each bob down with a slight tilt of your wrist or other movement of your hand. As Primo's head comes back up, return your hand to its original position. His head will move forward and back for all gaits except the trot or jog. That's how he counterbalances himself. He doesn't need to move his head for the trot because this gait automatically centers his balance. (See How to Post Primo's Long Trot in Chapter 6.) His head will bob for the walk, reach out for a lope and really stretch out for a full gallop.

When he reaches out more, you'll need to move your arms as well as your hands. For now, while Primo's just walking, concentrate on feeling how to keep your seat independent of your hands, so you won't hurt his mouth by using the reins to pull yourself back into position during faster moves.

Stopping Primo

After you've walked Primo a few hundred yards, and you've both gotten the feel of moving along together, it's time to stop him.

Before you stop Primo, make sure he's straight, not moving crooked or bending around a turn. Sit deeply and push your seatbones down into the saddle. Imagine that two of your friends have you by your arms and are trying to pull you forward. You really don't want to go, so you resist by dropping your weight down low. Use the same general idea to stop Primo. Drop your seatbones into Primo's back like a bee drops his tail to use his stinger. Brace with your legs, but don't squeeze Primo. Use a direct rein to pull back and slightly up. An upward lift of the wrist might be all the rein Primo needs. At the same time, say (and think) "Whoa." Use only as much rein pressure as it takes to do the job. Develop the habit of stopping Primo more with your body, primarily your seatbones and your legs, than with the reins. If cued correctly, he will stop on a loose rein. Rather than tug on his rein, think, think, think! This is the mark of a horseman.

Slow (check) Primo by using the same signals, only lighter. Say "Easy" rather than "Whoa" to check him.

If Primo doesn't respond to your seatbones, braced legs and a mild pull on the reins, try alternating them. For one-handed riding, move your fingers to jiggle the bit from side

Halt or Slow Down (Check)

Drop your seatbones into Primo's back like a bee drops its tail to use its stinger. Brace with your calves and use a direct rein, with the least amount of pressure possible. Develop the habit of stopping Primo more with your seatbones and legs than with your reins. Say "Whoa" only for stopping. Say "Easy" to slow or check Primo.

to side. One thing you must avoid is a steady hard pull on the reins. This only encourages Primo to lean into the bit and maybe even go faster. Some horses are trained to stop when you say "Whoa" and relax the reins instead of pulling them. Use the same leg/seat aids.

After you've stopped Primo, don't let him move again until you ask him. Experiment to find the least amount of pressure and manner of sitting required to keep Primo under control. Do not, however, do all your experimenting right away, and don't always stop him in the same spot. Whether you overdo or "always do," Primo will know you want him to stop and do it before you can ask him. This is called "anticipating." You must not let him pick up this habit.

Turning Primo

Resume walking and practice a few turns by neck-reining Primo. The moment Primo has turned as far to one side as you want, take the rein off his neck. Otherwise, he'll keep on turning. Horses that are hard to turn usually get this way after carrying riders who leave their "turn signals" on. Horses just learn to ignore the turn signals.

If you ride Primo two-handed, remember the experiment and be sure to pull only on the side you want him to turn. Release the pressure after he's turned enough.

Use your leg and body aids to signal turns. Just as Primo

For a simple turn to the right, lay the rein on the left side of Primo's neck. At the same time, apply leg pressure on his left side and take your leg off his right side. For two-handed reining, use a direct or open right rein and the same leg signals.

For a left turn, reverse all of the signals.

turns away from the rein's pressure for neck-reining, he'll also turn away from the pressure of your leg against his side. Simply press your calf against the side you want him to turn away from. At the same time, push out just enough on your other stirrup for your foot to point in the direction you want Primo to turn. For example, for a right turn, squeeze Primo with your left calf and point with your right foot.

This action should be a barely noticeable "scissor" of your legs. You don't need to strain and stick your leg out. Do not rotate your ankle to point your big toe. Remember what you learned by feeling your own seatbones move. Even a slight scissor is enough for Primo to feel your turn signal.

Before doing something new, practice turning and stopping Primo from a walk until you feel that he's responding smoothly to everything you ask for. Primo should:

- Stand quietly while you mount.
- Not move until you ask.
- Walk at a good tempo (speed) and not mope along.
- Continue to walk straight or along the fence line and at the same tempo until you stop or turn him.
- Stop promptly and calmly.
- Turn smoothly without resisting your cues.

Using Fences

Don't depend on a fence to turn or stop Primo. Fences usually *will* turn or stop Primo, which is why you should start out in an enclosed area. However, you must develop your own skills at turning and stopping him.

Some enclosures are round, others have corners. Right now, it really doesn't matter. For now just work on keeping

Primo about three feet from the rail. Don't let him drift in. Don't let him try to rub you against the rail, either. Later on, you'll use fences for practicing fancy moves. Turns are *basic* moves. Make Primo's turns your own idea, not just a matter of following your nose around a corner. Practice turns in the middle, not in the corners.

CHAPTER 6

---◆◄●►◆---

On Your Way

After you've ridden Primo at a walk long enough to feel confident about starting, stopping and turning him, you're ready to move on.

In order to look good together, you and your partner Primo need to move in unison. It's like dancing. When two people dance, both partners know the dance steps, but one partner leads. With riding, *you* do the leading while *Primo's* feet are the only ones on the dance floor. You *both* need to know the dance steps, that is, the gaits. Primo already knows them. Since you will do the leading, you need to learn them, too.

All Western horses use three gaits: walk, jog (trot) and lope (canter). Sometimes a gait will vary (say, for riding an American Saddlebred or a Tennessee Walking Horse Western style), but we'll concentrate on the Western walk, jog and lope. Primo's feet follow a particular footstep pattern for each gait. When riding a circle in either direction, *near* means Primo's "inside" feet and *off* are the "outside" ones. Riding a circle makes it easier for you to envision Primo's footfalls for the gaits. When you're not in a circle, *near* means the leading forefoot and the hind foot on the same side.

Gait patterns describe the order in which each foot hits the ground until all four feet have touched once to complete the cycle. Patterns are also made by sound, meaning the number of beats heard within each cycle. For example, if two feet land at the same time, that is considered one beat. You can also use the sound of feet hitting the ground to tell whether Primo is collected or extended in his gait. You mentally "draw" the sound. A "square" sound means he's evenly collected and "rectangular" sound means he's stretching out. A lopsided geometric figure can mean a problem, such as lameness.

The Walk

The walk is a four-beat lateral gait. In a lateral gait both feet on the same side touch before both feet on the other side. They land in this pattern: (1) near hind, (2) near fore, (3) off hind, and (4) off fore. Here are the tempos within the walk:

- Free walk—casual, unhurried and undriven. This is for resting or for getting past areas that seem suspicious to Primo.
- Medium walk—relaxed but slightly faster driven. This is Primo's best walk.
- Collected walk—obediently gathered up into the bit. The hindquarters reach under the body, and there's higher foreleg action. Actually, it's more suitable for a Western horse to be semicollected, because he's ridden on a looser rein.
- Extended walk—stretching out with lots of energy,

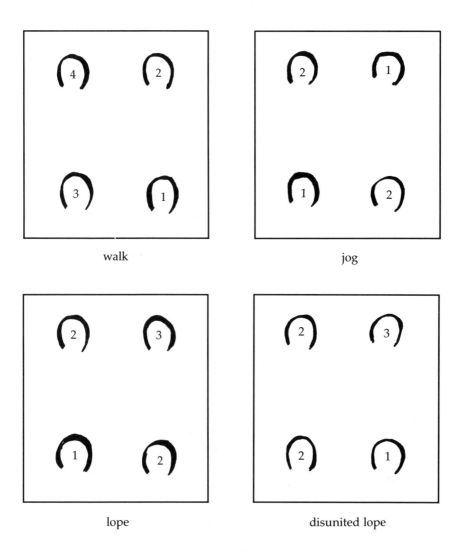

walk

jog

lope

disunited lope

Gait Patterns

Here are the patterns of Primo's footfalls for doing the walk, jog, lope and disunited lope in a clockwise direction (on his right lead).

Walk: (1) inside back, (2) inside fore, (3) outside back, (4) outside fore.

Jog: (1) inside fore and outside back, (2) outside fore and inside back.

Lope: (1) outside back, (2) inside back and outside fore, (3) inside fore.

Disunited lope: (1) inside back, (2) outside back and fore, (2) inside fore.

called impulsion. This is only used for exercising and to teach Primo to obey your cues.

The timing should be regular, with each foot clearly lifted. All gaits have similar tempos.

The rule book of the American Quarter Horse Association (AQHA) defines the walk for Western classes as "a natural, flat-footed, four-beat gait. The horse must move straight and true at the walk. The walk must be alert, with a stride of reasonable length in keeping with the size of the horse." (Primo's "stride" is the distance he covers each time he does one complete gait sequence, or pattern.)

Riding a Walk
Sunny rides Rooster two-handed in a good normal seat.

A good medium walk is very important. Each of the walk transitions is important. (A "transition" is the act of changing from one tempo or gait to another.) All too often, a horse's walk doesn't get the attention and practice that it deserves. Remember: if Primo can't do a good job at the walk, he surely can't do his best at the jog or lope.

The Jog

The jog (trot) is a two-beat gait that follows this sequence: (1) off hind/near fore, (2) near hind/off fore. The legs work together as opposites, or diagonals. The jog is a classic Western trot. It has a nice slow tempo and is the trot you would use for showing Primo unless the judge asked for more speed. Then you'd ask him for a regular trot. Primo's stride lengthens even more for the long trot (also called extended trot) and he covers more ground per stride, but his movements are slower because it takes longer for his hind legs to reach farther under him. Practice the long trot on soft ground. Hard or slippery footing can strain Primo's legs.

The AQHA rule book defines the jog as "a smooth, ground-covering two-beat diagonal gait. The horse works from one pair of diagonals to the other pair. The jog should be square, balanced and with a straight, forward movement of the feet. Horses walking with their back feet and trotting on the front are not considered performing the required gait. When asked to extend the jog, he moves out with the same smooth way of going."

The Lope

Think of the lope (canter) as a series of bounds. Three hoof-beats should be heard as the feet land in this sequence: (1)

off hind, (2) near hind/off fore, (3) near fore. If you hear four hoofbeats, then Primo is "hobbling" along rather than bounding. The only time you should hear four hoofbeats is when Primo is in a full racing gallop (running).

A disunited lope (also called a cross-canter or crossfiring) is how a dog lopes, but not a horse. If Primo crossfires, then he's "on his wrong lead." A disunited lope goes (1) near hind, (2) off hind/off fore and (3) near fore, compared to a regular lope's (1) off hind, (2) near hind/off fore, and (3) near fore.

Primo will be disunited while changing leads anytime he switches in front first. He'll switch legs in front in one stride and then in back on the second. This seldom happens when he lopes freely in the pasture because he'll pick the perfect moment to start his lope or to change directions while already loping. Sometimes he switches in front first because that is his immediate response to your cue to lope or change directions. He doesn't give himself time to "set up." Sometimes it's because he's lazy. If Primo continues to lope on the wrong lead, you'll feel an uncomfortable roughness through his back. You can see it, too. Look at his shoulders. If Primo's on the wrong lead, you'll see his outside shoulder stay slightly ahead of the inside one.

What do you do if Primo lopes on the wrong lead?

One thing you should *not* do is jerk him to a stop and discipline him. Let him lope for a few strides to see if he figures out what he's doing and changes on his own. If not, stop him, wait a moment, walk a straight line, and then ask him again for a lope.

The perfect moment for you to ask Primo to start loping or to change leads while loping is *when the front foot he's already leading with is on the ground.*

Most rule books, including that of AQHA, define the lope

as "an easy, rhythmical three-beat gait. Horses moving to the left should lope on the left lead. Horses moving to the right should lope on the right lead. Horses traveling at a four-beat gait are not considered to be performing at a proper lope. The horse should lope with a natural stride and appear relaxed and smooth. He should be ridden at a speed that is a natural way of going."

More About Leg Aids

Let's take a fresh look at three different leg areas that are used to signal Primo:

1. *Leg pressure* means pressing in with your calves. Your toes are forward and flexed upward, not rotated painfully outward. Leg pressure is used for turning, leg yielding and to ask for more speed. A trained Western horse normally moves *away* from your outside leg pressure, but sometimes he'll also use your inside leg for support as is done in English riding.

2. Your *seatbones* are part of your legs, too. Pressure from your seatbones is used for turning, leg yielding and to control Primo's speed. You use them to ask him to go faster or slower, to stop and to back up.

3. You use your *heel* (with or without a spur) to ask Primo for more speed, more energy or for a longer stride. Or, you might have to use your heel for turning Primo. Ideally, your heel is used only after your leg pressure is ignored. Press (don't poke) him by rotating your ankle.

Beware of constantly squeezing or constantly thumping on Primo's sides with your legs or feet to keep him going. Horses that are gentle enough for beginners to ride may be a bit lazy. If Primo's like this, with patience you can get him to wake up and move—even at a walk. This may take spurs. *Use each spur only when needed.* Use your seatbones, also. Remember what I said about rein signals in the last chapter? Don't leave your leg "turn signals" on, either. Once Primo learns to trust your leg aids as dependable messages, he'll respond to lighter signals.

How to Ride Primo's Jog

To ride Primo's jog, start out by walking. Ask him to increase his speed by whichever leg aid works best. If you use leg pressure, just flex your calves, don't squeeze your knees in. If you use your seatbones, as you squeeze your buttocks to roll your seatbones forward, you'll also feel the underside of your thighs flex against the saddle. (I personally prefer a horse that will move forward when I apply forward pressure with my seatbones.) You won't need to use calf pressure to drive a horse that responds to your driving seatbones. Save your calves for asking this nice horse to turn or for the lateral moves described later in this chapter.

Primo's response will tell you which leg aid he prefers. At the same time, raise the reins just a little. Lift the reins *up*, not *forward*, so the bit can contact Primo's mouth (or the hackamore can contact his nose) lightly to get his attention. If he doesn't respond, make your signals stronger and also nudge his sides with your heels. Test to find the lightest signals for doing the job. Your object is to keep your communications with Primo a secret from anybody who's watching. Think-talk helps, but you might need to get Primo's attention first. Go back to your normal seat position as soon as he reaches the jog.

All riding is a matter of balance. You need good balance

Riding a Jog
Teresa quietly sits upright in a normal seat for Pal's winning Western Pleasure jog. Pal's topline is relaxed.

Bo's feet and legs match Pal's. But compare the topline of both riders and horses. Cyrus leans forward as he posts Bo's jog, and Bo's neck is flexed as they pass Erin on C.J. Bo and C.J. are used for work and pleasure on the Jones cattle ranch. They are not used for competition.

to stay on Primo and he needs good balance to move with you on his back. How you use your aids affects balance. Your legs and body drive (push) Primo. Your hand on the rein restrains (pulls) him. Ideally, Primo is balanced between being pushed and being pulled.

With practice you'll be able to balance yourself on Primo's back almost as easily for a jog as for a walk. The trick is to give in slightly at your waist without bending forward. Stay loose, stay balanced and remember to *breathe*. The more you relax, the easier it will be to sit the jog. Picture your bottom "melting" into Primo's back, and let your "string" keep your upper body's blocks lined up. Keep enough contact with Primo's rein to be able to slow or stop him if he goes too fast.

How to Post the Long Trot

The Western term for a faster trot is "long trot." To ride it, you will need either to deepen your seat or to assume a forward position and "post." It's easier to post than to sit out a long trot.

To practice posting, stop Primo and count to yourself one, two/one, two. On the count of one, sit. On the count of two, push down in your stirrups to lift your weight just enough for your bottom to rise an inch or two off the saddle. On the next count of one, use your knees and ankles together as shock absorbers and return your weight gently to the saddle. Practice until you can count and move up and down smoothly and evenly as Primo stands still. (You'll use more muscles in your lower back and thighs for a forward seat than for a normal seat. If those muscles are weak or lazy, you'll have to work harder at first to post.)

Next, urge Primo into a long trot. Use the same aids to ask for a long trot as for a jog, only ask a little stronger.

Posting a Long Trot
Teresa posts Pal's long trot. Note Pal's relaxed topline.

Again, the horses' legs match. Sunny has to use more rein contact to control "red hot" Rooster's long trot. She sits nicely while posting and leans forward only very slightly.

When Primo's gait bumps you, let yourself go up and slightly forward. Then use your knees and ankles to control how you sit down again. When you rise, your shoulders should be just a few inches forward of your hips. You'll almost sit up straight, but don't lean forward too much, and do not squeeze. Instead of squeezing, flex your ankles and "lock" your knees. Use your knees for balance, but don't dig them into Primo's sides. Don't let your ankles swing forward and back each time you push up and come down. (Girls should not let their backs sway. They must remember to open their hip joints and use their posture muscles. Boys must try to keep their heels down.) Combine the "one, two" counting exercise you practiced while standing still with what you now feel when Primo jogs. This lets you find the rhythm. Now, work on making it smooth.

Practicing on a Lunge Line

A good exercise to help you find and improve your balance is to have someone lunge Primo while you ride him with no hands. Snap a rope at least fifteen feet long onto Primo's halter and ask a friend to work him in a circle at a long trot, preferably in a corral or other enclosed area. Primo should be worked in one direction and then the other. Six circles made in the same direction are plenty. Stop him and let him rest a moment before lunging him in the other direction. It's important not to lunge Primo too long because trotting in small circles is harder on his legs than trotting in larger circles.

Posting on a lunge line without hands teaches you that how you keep your body balanced and how you use your hands are two separate matters. In other words, one should not depend on the other. You *want* your hand to move back

Lungeing
Sunny posts Rooster's trot and "flies" while I lunge him.

and forth and "give in" as Primo bobs his head for balance at the walk and the lope. At the trot, however, he keeps his head steady. This is because his weight is already balanced by the diagonal foot patterns. When Primo trots, *you* are the only one who bobs.

If your hand bobs with you while you post Primo's trot, you'll jab him in the mouth at every stride. A good way to test your hand, to see if it's steady for using reins, is to stick your little finger down until it barely touches the saddle horn while posting Primo's trot. Ideally, you'll maintain a steady light touch.

Now that you know how to post Primo's long trot, you probably won't need to do it very often. If a Western rider wants to go faster than a walk or a jog, he or she generally lopes. Loping is more comfortable on both horse and rider.

How to Ride Primo's Lope

Ask Primo to lope the same way you ask him to move from a walk to a jog or a long trot (seatbones, and/or leg pressure and slight lift on the reins), only stronger. Learn to get Primo to lope both from a walk and from a jog. Experiment in an enclosed area to find out how strong you should signal him in order to go directly from a walk to a nice lope, and no faster. No gallop yet, please.

Remember how you'd sit on the rocking horse in your nursery? You'd work your waist muscles to make him really go back and forth. The same general idea applies to riding a lope, except that Primo does most of the work and you just flex your lower back to keep up.

When learning how to ride Primo's lope, you might find it easier to relax if you keep your feet a little more forward than you normally would. Use your waist to keep him rocking back and forth like your old hobby horse. As you rock, you'll automatically press into the stirrups with your feet. If you keep the ball of your foot on the stirrup (the way you should for safety reasons), your flexing ankles become involved. They send this rocking motion up through your legs to move your seatbones. When your seatbones move, Primo knows to keep on loping.

Once you get the rhythm of riding Primo's lope by the way just described, you need to make two corrections in order to avoid bad habits as an advanced rider. First, bring your feet back down instead of sticking them out forward, and second, don't rock backward with your body. After Primo starts to lope, straighten up and bring your feet down from out front to their usual position for a good normal seat. Let your feet drop so that your ankles line up with your hipbones. Keep your rocking confined to your lower back and pelvis area. Do not swing your legs back and forth.

Keep enough rein contact so that you can slow Primo down (check him) or stop him. Remember the signal. Drive down your seatbones, brace your legs and apply equal pressure on the reins. If necessary, pull-release-pull. Say and think "Whoa" to stop Primo and "Easy" to check him.

Again, think about using your body and legs more than your reins as brakes. Once Primo learns to trust your signals, he'll be more willing to stop on a loose rein.

In order to pick the right moment to ask Primo to lope on a particular lead, you have to know where his feet are. If he's already loping, you can tell whether it's his left or right lead by looking at his shoulder for a couple of strides. His

Riding a Lope
Pal is loping very nicely on his left lead. As they circle, Teresa looks ahead to where they're going.

When Rooster's lope feels rough, Sunny realizes that he's crossfiring. (Compare a proper lope with a crossfire on the gait chart.) Here she slows him to ask for a left lead.

Now she's straightened him out. He's loping nicely on his left lead as he continues to circle counterclockwise.

leading shoulder will stay slightly ahead of the other shoulder. Try to ask for a change of lead when his leading front foot is on the ground. Then he can get his hind foot ready to push off at a lope.

There's another way to tell which lead Primo's on, besides feeling how rough it is when he crossfires a lope. First, become familiar with the sequence of each gait. The pattern repeats itself for as long as he does that gait.

Next, teach yourself to recognize by feel which back leg Primo has down and which leg is up. You can do this at a walk. If at first you have trouble feeling it through the saddle, remove the saddle and ride Primo bareback (in the corral). Each time Primo raises his hind leg, the effort moves his body. You can feel his body's swinging motion under your legs. I may confuse you if I tell you how to "read" Primo's motion. It's easier to let you feel his moves for a while and read them your own way. Ask someone to watch and tell you if you're right while you call off "near leg," "far leg," "near leg" and so on each time you think that hind leg is up. You can call which one is down, if that's easier for you.

Primo's hindquarters are his driving force. That's why the sequence always starts with a hind foot (even though you may figure out his lead from watching his front foot). If you know the pattern, you'll also know which foot lands next just by feeling what his hind legs are doing.

Obviously it takes time to develop a feel for knowing where Primo has each of his legs. When you become involved in advanced riding, maybe even as a trainer, you'll need to locate each leg before asking Primo to make tricky moves. You'll be way ahead then if you start now to practice pinpointing Primo's feet from the saddle.

In his excellent book *Western Training: Theory and Practice,* Jack Brainard says, "To become proficient in applying diagonals and lateral control, there is one basic, all-important rule: Know where the horse's feet are. Know the location of his front feet while he is in motion, and his rear feet as well.''

Ideally, Primo should keep the same lead, gait and tempo until you ask him to change. Sometimes he changes leads on his own, without your asking. He may do it when he's loping on a long straightaway in order to rest the leg that's been leading. (Race horses do this.) If Primo uses one lead most of the time, that leg will become more developed than the other. You can help prevent this by working him equally on both leads. By working both leads, *you also* can stay flexible and not become one-sided.

Avoid unnecessary moves on Primo's back. If you twist your body around to look at something behind you or talk to somebody, Primo might take this to mean you want him to change leads or to turn.

Turning at a Jog or Lope

To turn Primo at a jog or lope, neck-rein him to the direction you want him to turn and at the same time push down in the stirrup *opposite* the side he'll be turning. (Do you recognize this ''scissor'' motion from learning turns at the walk?)

As you push on the stirrup, the resulting pressure that Primo feels on his side and back from your flexing leg and seatbone will probably be the only leg signal he needs to turn. He'll also feel your weight shift and want to move under it, but don't overdo these signals. Just let them happen naturally.

Depending on how he was trained, Primo might prefer different leg signals. Some horses turn easier if you slide your leg back farther behind the girth on the same side you want him to turn. He changes direction by making a turn on the forehand. (He'll swing his hindquarters out and turn in with his front end.) Whichever leg cue you use, combine it with the usual one- or two-hand rein signals.

How to Ride Primo in Circles

To start Primo in a circle, use the same signals you use for turning. Once he gets going, use only enough pressure to keep him turning and moving at the gait and tempo you want. How much pressure you use depends on how large you make the circle.

You might not think so, but actually you want Primo to travel straight when he goes in circles. "Straight" in this case means that his back feet follow (track) his front feet. It has nothing to do with the shape of his pattern, which may or may not be a straight line.

Primo might try to avoid making nice round circles the size you ask for. Sometimes, if he's not going straight, his outside hind foot steps wide of the circle. This puts extra strain on his inside front foot and throws him out of balance. Any time you feel Primo crowding in like this, you can encourage him to keep his circle big and round by leaning to the outside (keeping your shoulders level). He'll correct himself by moving his weight under you in order to keep his balance. You can also use leg pressure to move his hindquarters out or in more.

Primo might ease out and try to make his circles too big. If he does, lean slightly to the inside. If this doesn't work, neck-rein him a little to the inside. If he still goes wide—or if he *turns* in—ride two-handed and use a leading inside rein with an indirect outside rein. If he wears a curb bit, especially if the shank is one piece ("fixed") rather than loose, leverage from the shank will produce a stronger pull for a leading rein signal. As long as you don't pull hard, however, you can use two hands with a curb bit.

Ideally, you can control the size and shape of Primo's circles simply by using your weight and legs, and use the reins only to ask for changes in his speed or direction.

How to Back Primo

Before asking Primo to rein back (meaning to back up), he should be standing straight, not half-turned or crooked. Roll up on your seatbones and put more weight in your stirrups. Put equal weight in each stirrup. This is like asking Primo to stop, but with one big difference. To stop him, you deepen your seat, but to rein him back, you lighten your seat. Apply leg pressure behind Primo's girth on each side, giving a little squeeze on alternating sides. The easiest way to do this is just to alternate your weight in the stirrups. At the same time, hold the reins low, with equal pressure. Slowly say "Back." Primo should step back away from the pressure you give each side, which is why you apply it one leg at a time.

As soon as he moves, reward him by releasing the rein pressure and *maybe* your leg pressure. But do not change your seat. If Primo is well trained, he'll back straight for as long as you ask. Don't overdo it, though. Six or eight steps at a time is plenty. Then stop all pressure, sit in a normal seat and praise him. If he doesn't want to back at all, try again after making minor changes. Maybe you leaned your body forward instead of rolling up off your tailbone and up onto your thighbones' "fork." Try lifting the reins higher or

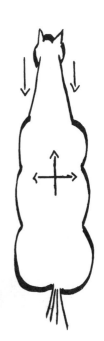

Backing Up

If Primo already knows how to back up, simply roll forward on your seatbones and ask him with direct reins, using mild pressure, possibly alternating and possibly adding leg pressure. Say "Back."

alternating them. Take your time. Be patient. Don't force the issue. If Primo doesn't back right away, but he does finally agree to take a step or two back, reward him by stopping the pressure. If he rears, runs backward or backs crooked, get help from an experienced rider before you try to back him again.

If he simply refuses to move back, you might be able to coax him at first from the ground. Stand at his head and lift the reins lightly. At the same time, push on his chest and say "Back." The moment he lifts a foot to step back, release your pressure on the reins and just barely keep contact on his chest. Then praise him for even one little step back.

Straight backing should be done quietly and without signs of resistance (such as opening his mouth to avoid the bit). Take it easy. Remember that Primo can't see where he's going for doing a rein back. This is why you should not back him in deep footing. He could stumble.

Leg Yielding

A leg yield is a lateral (sideways) move that's often used in Western riding. It means that the horse yields to pressure from your leg by moving away from it. It's used a lot in Trails classes and in other competition. It's handy for working ranch cattle, too. But it's also convenient for pleasure riding. For example, if Primo would move so you could open and shut gates from his back, you wouldn't have to dismount.

When asking Primo for lateral moves, it's better to use two hands (with a snaffle bit or hackamore) so that you can use a leading rein to coax him in a certain direction. Notice that I said "coax," not "pull." Lateral reining cues must be gentle. More signals are given with your legs and weight than with the reins. Plan all of your cues (hand, leg, body and especially think-talk) so that your suggestions add up to one command Primo clearly understands. Take your time. Be patient. Be clear. The moment you try to force Primo to make a lateral move by hauling hard on the rein, you've lost control.

Before you try leg yields from Primo's back, see how he responds when you stand next to him and push his side. He should yield and take a step sideways away from it.

Next, check the flexibility of Primo's neck when he responds to a leading rein by gently pulling his head around to either side by the rein on that side. Now mount him. Use a leading rein to ask him to bend his head back so that his nose nearly touches your boot. Do it from both sides. Keep your seatbones on "Whoa," otherwise Primo will think you want him to move. You might also need to keep a small amount of direct pressure on the other rein to prevent his moving.

Turn on the Foreleg

If Primo shows flexibility and moves away from a push on his side, it's time to try a lateral move from his back. The easiest and most useful one is a turn, or pass, on the foreleg. One of Primo's front legs should stay in place while he uses his hindquarters to move around it.

To turn around his right foreleg, apply leg pressure *behind* his right girth and turn his head with a leading right rein. Just tip his head, don't pull him. You want his hindquarters to move to the left and his right foreleg to stay in place. (Actually, he'll need to lift his right foot slightly several times as he turns, but he should put it back in almost the same spot.) Keep your left rein reasonably loose, unless you need

Turn Around the Right Foreleg
Apply leg pressure behind his right girth and turn his head with a leading right rein. You may need an indirect left rein. Raise your left leg barely off and scissor it slightly forward. That's the "open door" for Primo to move his hindquarters through. To pass around the left foreleg, do the opposite.

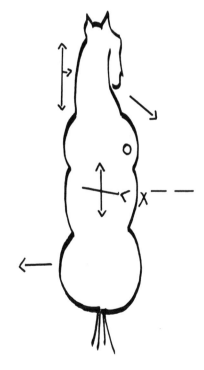

it to stop Primo from going forward. Barely raise your left leg and point it slightly forward. That's the cue Primo needs to move his hindquarters through. To pass around the left foreleg, do the opposite.

Turn on the Haunches

You can do a lot of things with Primo just by using a turn on the foreleg and a rein back. But you can do even more if he'll *turn on the haunches* (also called turn over the hocks), which is the opposite of a turn on the foreleg. One of Primo's back legs stays in place while he moves around it with his forelegs. It's easier, for example, to open and close a gate if Primo does all three moves.

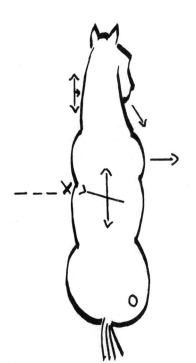

Turn Over the Right Hock
Start with a slight direct pull on the left rein to stop Primo's left front foot. Keep a little indirect pressure on that left rein as you give a leading pull on the right rein. Gently nudge Primo's left side several times with your leg at or just in front of the girth to move him. Lift your right leg and scissor it slightly back. This opens the door for Primo to walk around his right hock. For a turn over the left hock, do the opposite.

To coax Primo into doing a right turn on the haunches, start with a slight direct pull on the left rein. This gets his attention and should stop his left front foot. Keep a little indirect pressure on that left rein to discourage him from going forward. Then, immediately give a leading pull with the right rein. This starts the turn. Remember to coax, not pull, with the leading rein. Barely lift your right leg and point it slightly back. Apply on-off-on leg pressure to Primo's left side at the girth (the best place) or just in front of it (if needed). As you keep pressuring Primo's left side, he'll want to get away from it. The gentle reminder of the leading right rein and the shifted weight of your right leg should be enough to guide Primo to walk around his inside (right) hind foot. There you have it. For a left turn on the haunches do the opposite.

Sidepass

Next, you can ask for a *sidepass*. If Primo has been taught the sidepass, he likely learned it in stages. First he learned to turn on the foreleg, then he learned to turn on the haunches. A sidepass combines parts of both moves. Primo makes crossover steps directly out to the side, slowly and carefully, keeping his body straight.

To ask Primo for a sidepass to the right, sit straight in a normal seat and apply pressure at the girth with your left leg. At the same time, lift your right leg just enough to get its weight off Primo's side. Lift it straight out, not scissored front or back. Apply direct checking pressure on Primo's outside (left) rein and lead him to the right with an open rein.

Pressure from your left leg tells Primo to move. Your seat-bones shift as a direct result of your leg changes and give him the same message. But your balanced seat doesn't ask him to move forward or back. Your outside rein contact holds him from going forward, and your inside leading rein invites him to move to the right. Given this one clear choice, Primo should respond with a sidepass to the right.

At first, you might have to help Primo by facing a fence. Earlier I said not to depend on a fence to stop or turn Primo, but this is different. Until Primo understands what you want of him, a fence will keep him from going forward. "Over" is a good think-talk cue.

If Primo ignores your leg pressure, try bumping him with your leg. If he still ignores your leg, use your heel. Add a spur, if necessary, but give Primo a chance to respond to gentler aids before trying more severe ones.

You might have the opposite situation. Primo might be so highly trained in lateral work that these aids are too much.

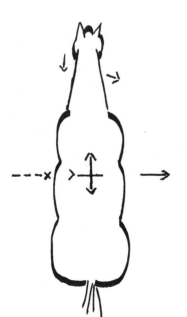

Sidepass to the Right
Apply a direct left rein to check Primo and lead him to the right with an open rein. Sit in a normal seat and apply pressure at the girth with your left leg. At the same time, lift your right leg straight out "to open his door." For a sidepass to the left, use the same signals and trade sides.

Two Track, Hindquarters Out to the Right

In the beginning, use a fence or something else solid. As Primo walks alongside the fence, apply an indirect left rein and ask him with your left leg to move his hindquarters to the right. At the same time, do not take your right leg off—don't give any pressure with it, either. Use your "scissored" seatbones to drive him forward. You want Primo to go straight by making two paralleling sets of tracks. To signal him to swing his hindquarters out to the left, trade everything right for left. Once you and Primo get your signals clear, you won't need a fence.

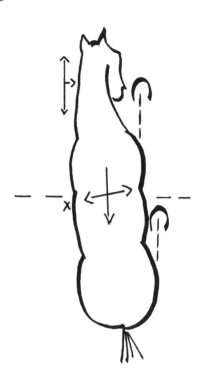

If he already has "power steering," all you need to do is steady him with the reins, one-handed, to keep him from going forward or back. Your leg and weight aids stay the same, and you definitely won't need a fence.

If you've had success so far, you eventually might like to try some more lateral moves with Primo.

Two-Track

If you can get Primo to turn around his foreleg, you probably can get him to *two-track*. When Primo moves straight forward, with his back feet following his front feet, he makes two tracks. For a *two-track*, however, Primo's back legs move in a different set of tracks than his front legs while he goes forward. When he two-tracks, he really makes four tracks. They should all be parallel.

Start out by using a fence. Get Primo moving forward along the fence. Now use leg pressure behind his girth on the outside (next to the fence) to ask him to move his hind-quarters to the inside (away from the fence). At the same time, shorten your outside rein. Keep your inside leg on Primo's side, but don't give any pressure with your inside leg or the inside rein. Think-talk what you want him to do.

The Rollback

The *rollback* is a 180-degree (half a circle) turn over the hocks. Although it can be done at the trot, generally a rollback is much faster. Primo lopes or gallops up to a point, stops, lifts both front feet to turn over his hocks and lopes back down the same path. You'll probably see Primo do a rollback on his own when he's just burning off steam in the round-pen.

Do not try a rollback right away. It's not for beginners. If Primo tries a rollback on his own, without your asking, your defense against falling off is three-stage: (1) counterbalance yourself by pushing on the stirrup on the same side he's turning, then (2) push on the opposite stirrup to stay with him and meanwhile (3) grab the saddle horn.

The Spin

Keep up the pressure of a turn on the hocks and you have a *spin*. That's where Primo makes one or more complete circles with his front feet while keeping one back foot in place to pivot around.

A spin does not need to be fast. In fact, most problems

occur because the horse feels rushed while doing a spin. Rather than take a series of crossover steps, he rears up and hops around. The only time Primo should rear slightly is for a rollback. In a correct spin, Primo's body is straight. Only his head and neck are tipped to the inside. He stays flat (no dropped shoulder) and calm. You can work Primo up to a spin by riding him in circles that get smaller and smaller. Eventually, he'll find it easier just to plant a back leg, use his other back leg for counterbalance, and make crossover steps with his front legs to pivot around the supporting back leg.

For your safety and Primo's, *do not* try any lateral work at a gait faster than a walk for quite a while. There's more to consider than simply how it's done. For example, Primo has to be in good condition. Otherwise, he can pull a muscle or tendon, or even break a leg. It takes a lot of work on a regular basis for both horse and rider to get in condition. Also, the condition of the ground is important. If its too hard, too soft or too deep, Primo can hurt himself. Finally, before Primo does reining and cutting moves like sliding stops (which I intentionally did not describe), rollbacks and fast spins, he needs special shoes (called slider plates, or sliders) on his back feet. All of these moves that I hint about but don't describe in this book will be explained in my next book. *Western Performance: A Young Rider's Guide* is for the more advanced rider.

How to Reverse Primo

When you reverse Primo, you turn him around and head back in the other direction. There are several ways to do this. The easiest way is to make a U-turn at a walk. Just neck-rein him and use your leg to turn him. Signal him long enough for him to turn all the way around. The next easiest way is for Primo to make a turn on the foreleg, which is described on page 135. This can be done at a walk or a jog. Another way is a turn over the hocks, which is described on pages 136–137.

How to Go Through a Gate

If you ride in a Trails class at a show, you'll lose points if you can't go through a gate by opening and closing it from Primo's back. If you leave a gate to the pasture open and the cows get out into the neighbor's garden, you'll probably lose more than points! Gates generally are kept shut except when someone needs to pass through.

There are several correct ways to go through a gate on Primo. When the gate opens *away* from you, the easiest way (assuming your left hand is your rein hand) is to use a right-hand *push*. If the gate opening is on the left, here's how to do it:

- Approach the gate from the right so that Primo is parallel to it. Move him slowly forward until his head is just past the latch, then stop him. Reach over and unlatch the gate.
- Back Primo a step or two and push the gate partly open. Do not remove your hand from the gate.
- When Primo's head clears the gatepost, turn his head into the opening and walk him through. Your hand will automatically open the gate wide enough for Primo to pass through the opening.
- When your right leg is on the other side of the gate, use that leg to push Primo's hindquarters around to the left (a turn on the foreleg).

- Use your left leg to move his front end over to the right to get him straight.
- Ask Primo for a step or two forward to get closer. Then shut and latch the gate. Praise Primo for a job well done, and continue your ride.

On your way back, you'll need to *pull* the gate open. Here's how to do it.

- Line up with the gate so that it's parallel, but basically in front of you, with the latch at your left leg.
- Unlatch the gate with your left hand and pull it toward Primo. Back him a step.
- Use your left leg to turn his hindquarters to the right for a quarter circle. This will arc him around the gate so that he faces the opening.
- Walk him forward until his back leg clears the gate.
- Move his hindquarters to the right with your left leg until he's parallel with the gate. Ask him to back a step or two so that you can latch the gate.

If a gate fastens on the right, do everything on the left. You'll find other ways to open and pass through gates. For example, Primo might prefer to back through, then turn.

Putting It All Together

You now have enough riding information about yourself and Primo to put him through almost any pattern at any gait just by fitting all the right pieces together. At this time, however, you probably have more information stored in your *head* than in your *body*. Real knowledge will only come from experience. You need to try things out and to practice the things you've learned:

- Making large and small circles.
- Figure eights and serpentines (zigzags). Practice turns, checks, stops and reverses.
- Backing and leg yielding.
- Changing gaits.
- Staying in the same gait and changing tempo.
- Opening and closing gates.

Developing a "Take-Charge" Attitude

In the first chapter, I said that a rider might become afraid to try something new, even after he or she rides well enough, because the rider lacks the experience to meet the challenge. Next to practice, a take-charge attitude is a rider's strongest defense against trouble. A positive, confident attitude is communicated to Primo as readily as fear or uncertainty.

I've already said how important it is for you to relax while riding Primo, but until now it's been in terms of getting your body lined up properly. But there's another important reason you need to be relaxed. When you feel threatened, your muscles get tense in your neck, jaw, shoulders and buttocks. Primo is sensitive to this and he reacts by tensing his own neck, jaw, shoulders and hindquarters.

You can't give good aids when you're tense, and Primo can't feel your aids as well when he's tense. This means that when you get tense, you lose some control. Without control, it's easier for you and/or Primo to panic and forget your training. (This is a good reason not to put a beginning rider with a green horse. It is the *main* reason to have someone with you—to be there in case of an emergency.)

As you've discovered, you're more relaxed while doing something familiar than when you do something for the first time. By planning your lesson of the day, you'll know what's supposed to happen when you ride. Then you can take charge and lead Primo through the course. When you're already relaxed and confident of what *should* happen, you'll be in better condition to handle something unexpected.

Draw up some lesson plans for riding Primo. Work out several lessons at a time. Write them down and carry your plan of the day with you when you ride.

Like you, Primo is more relaxed when doing something familiar. Even for things he's already been trained to do, he may not have done those things for *you*. Since there's more than one way to ask a horse to do anything, you will have to let Primo learn your way.

You know by now not to abuse Primo with the reins, but keep in mind that anytime you use leg aids, you must avoid steady pressure against his sides. Don't leave your "turn signals" on and don't *clamp* with your legs. You want a soft-sided horse that is truly responsive to your leg cues. Constant pressure with the legs, however, makes this impossible. It's much better to tap with your leg than to lock it against Primo's side. Tap, wait for a response and tap again rather than clamp. If you don't need your leg, keep it off Primo's side. (By that I mean "no pressure.")

When planning your lessons, always include the basics and add a little something new whenever you feel ready. Build slowly. If ever there is a problem, stop the lesson and wait for another time to try it. (Make this seem to be *your* idea, not Primo's.) Do *not* stop riding on that bad note, however. Go directly into riding something you know you can do well together. *Then* you may stop.

If Primo does something wrong or doesn't do what you

ask when you're riding him, it is likely that he's responding to something *you* did wrong in the first place. Or, you may not be asking him correctly. Read and study before you try again at whatever Primo "failed" to do. If necessary, get help and advice from an experienced rider instead of getting into a fight with Primo.

No one likes to be nagged and neither does Primo. If you go over and over something he's doing wrong, he'll get bored and simply ignore you. Keep riding fun for both you and Primo.

CHAPTER 7

———◆◆◆———

Pleasure and Practical Riding

One way to keep riding fun for both you and Primo is to do something different and not just practice in an arena or corral. It's good to move out of the arena, at least some of the time. Remember to bring a friend along, and/or to tell someone where you plan to ride.

Riding Along Roads

In most parts of the country a horse has the legal right-of-way over a car. However, most drivers don't know it or don't care. If you must ride along a road, stay where you and Primo are most visible to traffic and have the most room to get out of the way in an emergency.

Find out how Primo feels about cars *before* you ride along a road. Most horses are used to cars, but some are afraid of them. A horse that fears cars can never be trusted to carry a youngster anywhere near traffic. Before getting into real traffic, you can find out about Primo and cars by having someone drive a car past you while you ride. Have the test car pass you in both directions and honk the horn, too.

Notice how Primo acts when the car comes up behind him and when it comes toward him. See if he strongly reacts to one or the other approach. If he's pastured near a busy road or highway, you can watch his reactions to the traffic from the pasture or while you ride him in the arena or corral.

If a road has a lot of traffic, it will probably have a shoulder, and you can ride there. But be careful. Shoulders are often littered with broken glass and other objects that can injure Primo.

Realize that anything Primo sees as a threat to his safety can be dangerous. "Horse eaters" include dogs, chickens, laundry flapping on clotheslines, signs and billboards, bridges, drainage ditches, boxes, blowing paper, even cattle. (Even though Primo is a Western-trained horse, there is no guarantee that he likes cows.)

He does, however, need to get used to new situations. You make a mistake if you go to the other extreme and never ride Primo anywhere new. Without some variety in routine and scenery, he'll become "barn sour" and never want to leave home. Expose him to new sights, sounds and smells. If Primo seems afraid of something that looks ordinary and harmless to you, stop and show it to him. Let him learn that it's not a threat. Unless he gets panicky and becomes too dangerous, stay in the saddle. If he shies (starts suddenly aside) you'll have better control over him when you're on his back. You might get knocked down if you dismount. Or you might just have a long walk home alone. After Primo shows any sign of accepting the problem, praise him and continue on past. If he shies away from another object on the way back, stop and let him study it. Maybe he didn't notice it when he went by the first time.

Primo doesn't see or learn quite the same way you do.

For one thing, he sees a different picture with each eye. Primo sees a broader area than you do. Nature gave this ability to his ancestors so they could see enemies coming from any direction and take flight. He gets a general picture of everything except what's directly in front of him or what's directly in back of him when his head is down for grazing. He doesn't see as clearly as you do because his eyes are too far apart for him to be able to focus both eyes on one object. Things that *move* are more obvious to Primo. He sees motion, but he may not see what *causes* it. So he might shy at a piece of paper blowing in the breeze.

Also, Primo's brain works in a different way from ours. The right side of a horse's brain learns only what it *sees* from his left eye, and the left side of the brain learns from his right eye. Information brought in by Primo's other senses *is* shared, but the right and left sides of the brain cannot share information regarding vision. Therefore, even if a horse sees a problem the first time, he might have seen it with only one eye. He can honestly react to seeing the same thing with the other eye for the first time.

Always give him a chance to check out with *both* eyes what he might have seen with only one eye before. Then use a no-nonsense tone of voice (no shouting) and maybe a crop or spur to back up your leg and rein aids, if he doesn't want to walk past something.

If Primo still won't go forward to pass something he's afraid of, you need to change your strategy. Make him reverse and then back him all the way past it (on his "good eye's" side). Or go around it. Whatever you do, keep returning to the "monster" until passing it is no longer a problem. Use think-talk now if you haven't already tried it. Stay calm and don't give up until Primo accepts the monster.

Then reward him. A spoiled horse is not fun and can be dangerous. (Read Chapter 9, What Is Primo Thinking? for more information.)

In places where the shoulder is next to unfenced fields or nice lawns, show respect to the landowner and stay off the property. It might have seeds planted for crops (which you can't see yet) or have crops already growing. In either case, riding can do damage. Since a field is usually plowed under after the crop has been harvested, you would not damage anything by riding in it then.

Plowed fields have long rows called furrows. Because the ground line zigzags regularly, it's ideal to practice riding. Staying in the "valley" part would keep Primo in a nice straight lope. You could work on an even stride by riding him crossways, stepping over and between each "hill" part of the furrow. If the field has been harrowed or disked (so that it's level and soft, like a deep arena), you could put Primo through his patterns using different gaits and then check his footprints to see how he places his feet.

If your heart beats faster every time you pass a big, unfenced field, ask the owner for permission to ride there or perhaps on the road along its edge. Cultivated fields usually have dirt roads (called turnroads) for the farmer to use for taking his truck to check on the crops.

Besides the luxury of having lots of room, one of the best things about riding in fields and turnroads that are plowed or disked regularly is the lack of holes and big cracks that Primo might step in and twist or break a leg. Natural land and even some pastures can have bad holes, deep cracks and gullies from drought and erosion. I don't want to scare you away from having a good lope across the prairie. As long as you watch the ground ahead of you, you'll be all right.

If you convince the farmer that you will keep Primo out of his crops, he'll probably give you permission to ride on his land. A landowner might let you ride on his property that has a fence and gates if he's assured that you'll close all gates *immediately* after you. You should not pass along the permission given to you to other riders. Let them ask for themselves.

By the way, cows, sheep and goats are generally peaceful. They might be curious, but they'll keep their distance. One exception is a cow that's trying to protect her calf. She can be worse than a supposedly mean bull. If a landowner keeps horses in his pasture, *stay out*. Otherwise, you could get hurt when the horses come over to Primo. There's almost always some squealing and kicking during the "introductions." Stay away from donkeys, mules and ponies, too. In fact, Primo should not be allowed to socialize nose-to-nose over a fence with any strange horse that you meet along the road. The other horse might carry an infectious disease, which Primo could catch simply by greeting the sick horse.

Road Safety

Safety is very important on the road. Wear a hard hat and something colorful and bright. You want drivers to see you easily. Don't ride along roads at night or at any time when it's hard to see. Stay away from the road when you know there's going to be more traffic than usual (for example, at the end of a work shift at a nearby factory or after a ball game at a nearby stadium). Decide which side of the road you'll use ahead of time. If you must cross over to the other shoulder, don't cross near a blind turn. Cross only where you can *see and be seen* by traffic. Leave yourself enough

Riding Along a Road
Cyrus, Erin and I ride along the better shoulder of a curvy country road. We are wearing hats and colorful clothes and are being extra cautious as a car passes us.

space and time to get across safely or else to return and wait safely.

If you must cross a busy road, it will be safer to dismount and lead Primo across. Roads can be slippery. With you on his back, the footing could be bad for Primo. He could slip and panic. If he does this when a car was very close to you, you must turn him loose to save yourself. In any emergency, your own safety comes first. Besides, Primo might make it across to the other side better on his own.

Riding the Trails

Riding Primo out in the wide open spaces, through the woods or along a mountain trail can be a wonderful experience. If there are no mountains or woods nearby, you can probably find a field just up the road. That will do fine.

Pleasure riding can be either challenging or relaxing. Either way, it's supposed to be pleasant. You and Primo are out to have a good time. If you follow a few important rules or guidelines, your ride will be pleasant *and* safe.

• The first rule is to begin and finish slowly, no matter what kind of a ride you take. Give Primo a chance to loosen up and get his blood circulating before you ride any faster than a jog. Never lope back to the barn or return from a pleasure ride with a hot horse. Walk for the final ten minutes. That's usually long enough to cool Primo down. Sometimes it's better to dismount, loosen the girth and spend those last ten minutes leading him back to the barn.

If Primo doesn't want to walk back to the barn and dances around, he might think that your getting off is his reward for misbehaving in this manner. You don't want him to think this. Bring him to a full stop for a moment, then ask him for a walk. If he starts dancing again, stop him. Keep this up until he accepts your orders. You may have to take a short sidetrip or go back up the trail far enough to make your point and give him time to stop sulking. Try stopping along the way to let him graze. You can do this if he is not wearing a complicated bit. Otherwise the grass will get tangled in his mouthpiece. (A grazing bit is fine.)

• What should you do if you find yourself in heavy brush that blocks your path? Before you try to go through, check for thorns, wasp nests, old fence wire and snakes. If it looks passable, cup yourself over Primo's neck, grab the horn and

Going Through Rough Areas
Cyrus leans low over Bo's neck and gives him free rein to find his way through the low branches and up the steep bank that's full of rocks. Erin and C.J. await their turn on the other side of the creek.

hold onto your hat if it is not held in place by a chinstrap. Shield your eyes, slacken the reins and let Primo slowly find his own way through. (This sort of situation comes up when you're rounding up cattle, too. Some cows take their calves and hide in rough brush. You and Primo really have to work at coaxing them out to join the rest of the herd.)

If you're in a group and someone offers to hold a branch to one side, say no, thank you. Usually you can just let the branch brush over your back and Primo's or hold the branch for yourself, from start to finish. If someone accidentally lets go too soon, the branch could knock you off Primo.

• Whether you're in the saddle or on the ground, keep

away from cactus, big rocks and fallen trees. You or Primo could get stuck or bruised. More serious, these are favorite hiding places for snakes, spiders and scorpions—all best to avoid.

• Sometimes you'll find a field that looks abandoned. Look for a "No Trespassing" sign. If you can't find one, and if there are no houses nearby (where the owner might live), you might want to explore. You'll probably find broken fence posts and pieces of old wire stuck in trees. This is from where the trees grew around the wires long after the fence fell into ruin. Look out for wire that is partly buried or hidden in brush.

If the field looks like a good place to visit on a regular basis, you should walk through and inspect it before you "claim" it for riding. If you come across a dangerous place, mark it with a stick or something that you can find next time. Next visit, carry some strips of bright fabric in your pocket. Find each marker and tie a strip to it so it can be seen from horseback to warn you and other riders of the wire, broken post, hole or whatever.

There is a safe way to cross the wire with Primo, if it's low and loose enough. Dismount and show him the wire. Hold your foot over the wire until he gets across. Give him enough rein and pat his rump. He'll understand and go.

• You know not to deliberately ride fast over strange ground unless you can clearly see that there are no holes, stumps or other obstacles ahead. But sometimes you don't have a choice. Primo might run away with you. If this happens, neck- or lead-rein him to whichever side has the most space for you to circle him without crashing into something or running onto a road. He'll have to slow for circling. Then you can use a pulley rein, your legs and seatbones to stop him.

• Never punish Primo for running out of control. It will only add to his confusion. Chances are, he was just as scared as you while he ran. If possible, turn him around and slowly return to where the trouble started. Stop him and take a few moments to settle you both before going on.

• If an unmannerly horse such as a kicker or biter is part of a group ride, the owner should warn the other riders not to follow the horse too closely. (After you learn how horses talk, you can usually spot a potential troublemaker.)

• If someone in your group has a problem with controlling his or her horse, don't make it worse. Coming up from behind any horse and rider and charging past is bad manners at any time. But it's downright dangerous if the horse is already giving problems. Don't take off on Primo and leave the other rider behind. Don't even speed up without first telling the rider what you plan on doing. Having Primo get ahead might be all the horse needs at that point to explode.

Be an unsung hero. If the rider says he or she needs help, or if you sense it, stay behind while the others lope on. Use Primo to help calm the other horse, not to challenge him. Meanwhile, you'll help calm the other rider. You may need to hold the other horse's rein, but it's seldom a good idea to dismount. An exception would be if the other rider were thrown. Should this happen, don't take off after the runaway. It's more important that you stay with the rider, who may be injured. Let the other riders round up the loose horse when it catches up with them.

• If Primo gets excited when you ride in groups, switch to a more severe bit for those rides. Do the same if he forgets his manners whenever he gets out of the arena and into the wide open spaces. More bit is safer for you and kinder to him than sawing on his mouth for control.

• Think about how Primo feels. If you're hot, tired or thirsty, he probably is, too. Stop and rest. Move into the shade. Find water for him. He'll thank you for it.

How to Handle Hills

You've learned how important it is for your center of balance to match Primo's. Now let's think about balance in terms of riding him up and down hills.

Notice as you walk up a flight of stairs. Your balance shifts slightly forward, doesn't it? It'll shift forward slightly *more* if you swing your arms to match strides with your legs. You'll notice that it's easier to walk up stairs when you swing your arms rather than keep them down at your sides.

When you get to the top, turn around and walk back down. Did you shift your weight back for this? No, you didn't. If you did, you'd fall backward unless you held the rail. You kept your body straight for counterbalance. You also shifted more weight to your knees for coming down.

How about your arms? Did you pump them forward, or keep them down? You kept them down. You didn't need their weight in motion this time. In fact, that would have thrown you too far forward.

Apply what you discovered with the stairs to what you need to do in order to help Primo go up and down hills. You'll need to balance yourself the same way on his back as you did when you were climbing up and down yourself. You'll counterbalance with more weight above your waist when Primo climbs and more weight at your knees when he descends. Instead of swinging your arms, you'll hold them steady at his neck. You'll hold them higher up his neck when he climbs than when he descends.

Riding Up Hill
I've leaned in a forward seat and given Spot plenty of rein so that he can pick his way up this rocky slope. Spot is willing to try anything, but he's a very cautious climber.

You'll need to sit in a forward seat for two reasons. First, to make it easier for *you* to climb and descend. Second, to get your weight off Primo's loins so he has more freedom to use his powerful hindquarters.

When Primo goes up a hill, he swings *heavier* (but not *more*) with his neck to help himself climb, just as you swing your arms to help yourself climb. Assume a forward seat and keep yourself lined up like you're climbing the same hill Primo climbs. You'll naturally push down and back on the stirrups, with your legs practically straight. If the hill is quite steep, Primo's neck will be up high enough for you to

As Spock and I climb the trails on our place, I prepare for a much steeper rise. Big bold Spock wants to charge up full speed, rocks or no rocks. Knowing this, I hold mane and rein with one hand so I'll have something to grab for the climb, and I use the other rein to control his speed.

grab a handful of mane for support. Mane is fine for this purpose. Rein is not.

Picture yourself walking down the hill, step for step, with Primo. You'll still use a forward seat. Your feet will push slightly forward because of the added weight you'll naturally shift to your legs for counterbalance. Remember not to lean back. Keep your chin and shoulders level.

Use your leg aids to keep Primo straight. If either end swings out, he'll be off balance. You don't want Primo two-tracking down a hill. Use your leg behind the girth to push him straight again. Hold the horn to keep your balance when you move your leg back. Remember that Primo's driving

Riding Down Hill

I'm not *leaning* forward, but I've shifted my *weight* forward onto my knees and thighs. I'm also asking Spot, who is now two-tracking, to swing his hindquarters more to the right.

Spock and I come back down the hill. This is a pretty good example of what both horse and rider should do.

power is in his hindquarters even when he's on level ground. Right now, his hindquarters have extra driving power from his lumbosacral joint being flexed. It's his hindquarters, therefore, that need to be kept straight. Don't even bother using the reins to straighten his front end. Use the reins just to turn him if the trail turns, or if you need to go around something.

Sometimes you'll have to cross some rough gullies or ravines. Use the same methods just described for handling hills. Take your time and stay calm.

Climbing and descending require that you and Primo work well together. You've got to team up and align yourself with him. You've got to trust his surefootedness. If you start worrying, you'll tense up. As you already learned, getting tense causes you to lose control. Primo's got to trust you to keep your body positioned to counterbalance his weight shift. Otherwise, your misplaced weight will throw him off far easier than if he were carrying you on level ground.

Before Riding Primo into Water

Horses enjoy playing and working in and around water. You'll love riding Primo in water, especially at the beach. As with any kind of riding style, safety is vital.

If you don't live near a saltwater beach, try a lake or a river. Before you and Primo head out to the nearest body of water, make sure it's legal for you to ride him there. If private property is involved, be sure to ask the landowner for permission.

Wherever you go for water, investigate it first. Be especially suspicious of any areas where you can't see the bottom. Primo could get hurt by broken glass, tree stumps, rocks, wire and other objects that are submerged in the water or buried under a thin layer of sand or mud. He could get tangled in underwater weeds or submerged cable. He could get stuck in quicksand or similar sticky footing. He could lose his balance in a strong current, or he may not be able to climb a steep, slippery bank to shore.

You'll find most of these hazards around smaller lakes, rivers and ponds rather than on ocean beaches or beaches next to big lakes. Although cans and broken glass often hide in the dunes, most beach trash gets carried out by the tide. The beach has other problems, however.

- Watch for drivers who don't realize that a horse has the legal right-of-way. It's better to move over or wait for a vehicle to pass than to risk getting hit.
- Watch for swimmers or sunbathers who don't realize that a horse weighs half a ton and won't get out of your way. Or they may even come closer, wanting either to pet Primo or ride him. This could frighten Primo.
- Watch for sailboats, windsurfers, surfers on boards and fishermen who have lines out. Even if they see you and want to move, they may not be able to get out of your way in time. Beware also of kites, Frisbees and motorcycles when you ride on the beach. Leave yourself room for error. Primo might be busy with what's happening and not respond as quickly to your signals.
- Get out of and away from the water immediately if lightning threatens. Head back home.

Introducing Primo to Water

When you introduce Primo to the water, it's best to go with a rider and horse who are familiar with the beach. If this is the first time for Primo, he might not want to get his feet wet. Stay on his back, though. Give him a loose rein and plenty of time to look at the water and explore its sounds and smells before coaxing him in. Realize that, because of his poor vision, he doesn't know how deep it is. All he has to go by is its feel. And it feels strange! Even the ground next to the water feels different.

Once Primo realizes that the water won't pull his feet out from under him, he'll probably decide to venture in. But he might back out fast, once or twice, so be prepared. Keep calm and hold either the horn or a handful of mane.

Entering Water for the First Time

C.J. backs out as Erin asks him to enter the pond. He'd probably have gone on in this time if she'd asked him more firmly. Bo, on the other hand, acts like he's nailed to the ground. He ignores Cyrus's signals and refuses to go any closer to the water.

So we got Spot to go in. Now C.J. and even Bo are willing to follow. As he goes into the water, C.J. is asking Erin for more rein slack. He wants to test the water with his muzzle and maybe take a drink. Rather than take a chance on getting soaked, cautious Erin keeps a firm contact on the rein. She knows that once they've tested the water, some horses like to lie down in it!

Beach Workouts and Water Therapy

You might want to use a nylon bridle around the water because saltwater can ruin leather. (If you clean and condition the leather immediately after it dries, however, the damage will be less.) Wear boots and use a saddle when riding in water that doesn't go above Primo's knees. If you use the beach for exercising Primo, the best times to do this are early mornings and off-season. At other times the beach is usually too crowded for long lopes.

After the ride, you can use water to relax Primo while you bathe him. Remove the saddle and lead him out to knee-deep water. Once he's used to it, he'll stand contentedly while you pour buckets of water over his body and massage his favorite (or sore) spots.

Sand and Sea

Some horses enjoy rolling in shallow water. Rolling in the water can be as much fun for you as for Primo. Keep his reins or lead line free, however, or he can get tangled.

Primo can get sunburned on his white areas. Your own waterproof sunscreen will protect Primo from sunburn, but not from sunstroke. Don't overdo your fun in the sun! Take him into the shade for a break at least every half hour.

Horses can wet their lips in saltwater, but they should not be allowed to drink it. Most won't even try. A horse must drink water, however, to survive. Dehydration brought on by sweat is just as possible on the beach as in the desert. As a rule, Primo can drink lake or river water. If the water's not safe, or if you plan on being at the beach for more than a couple of hours, bring along a big jug of drinking water for Primo. Make it a rule to offer *him* water whenever *you* get thirsty.

Deep Water

You and Primo can have lots of fun without getting into deep water. In fact, you need never go any deeper than up to your knees. *Do not try swimming with Primo unless you are a strong swimmer. And, as all good swimmers know, bring a buddy.* In this case, the buddy should be an adult who is also a strong swimmer. A strong swimmer should *at least* be able to swim five hundred yards and tread water for thirty minutes. If you can do this, and if you can stay on Primo without a saddle, here's what will happen when you wade in deeper.

As the water reaches halfway up Primo's body, you'll feel him start to lose his footing. Sit in a forward position and

Swimming With Primo in Deep Water

First of all, give Primo a loose rein so he can use his head for balance. Hold on to his mane or a neck strap. Get a good hand grip, because you won't be gripping with your legs. Lean forward and arch your back slightly. Let the water lift you off Primo's back so that you float. Spread your legs and straddle him loosely. You'll be above (but not on) his back. Steer by flexing *your* back from side to side.

give him plenty of rein, so he'll be free to bend his lumbosacral joint and use his head and neck for balance. You won't have stirrups to help you balance, and it does get slippery in the water without a saddle. Grab a handful of mane. If Primo's mane is roached, use a neck strap.

Whether you're in a flowing river or the ocean, don't let Primo get crosswise to a strong current. (If you're crossing a flowing stream, go *with* the current. Cross on a slant instead of going straight across.)

As the water gets deeper, Primo will be partially supported by the water. By the time it reaches halfway up his body, you'll feel him start to propel himself by pushing off the bottom.

When the water is deep enough to pass over Primo's back, it'll lift him and he'll start to swim. Actually, at this depth, he'll do a combination of swimming and pushing off the

166

bottom. *That's deep enough*, though. Don't take chances and let him go any deeper. If, by accident, you and Primo get into deep water, *don't panic*. Use this same method to stay on Primo while he's swimming in water barely over his back or in water much deeper.

Holding on to his mane, spread your legs and arch your back slightly. Lean forward and let the water lift you off Primo's back so that you float. Don't move your position. You'll straddle Primo's back. You'll be above, but not on, his back. Steer by flexing *your* back from side to side. Stay over Primo and let him tow you by your grasp on his mane or neck strap. This position is much safer than swimming alongside him. You won't get in the way of his legs and feet.

If you get washed off and can't pull yourself back into position using Primo's mane or strap, keep hold of his mane or strap with one hand. Push against Primo with the other hand. This puts your body at an angle to his shoulder and keeps you out away from his feet. Hold that position until you can regain footing. Then either remount or lead (or follow) him out of the water.

If Primo panics while in the water, you should try to stay on. It's safer on his back. The only time you should bail off is if your weight seems to interfere with his efforts to recover. If Primo falls, or you fall or bail off, get *completely* out of his way. Let Primo try to save himself. Unless he's trapped or exhausted, he should be able to get out by himself. Horses are natural swimmers. And regardless of how much you love Primo, your own safety *must* come first.

Accidents seldom happen if you follow the rules and use common sense. Even so, you *must* use the buddy system when you take Primo to the water. It's safer and also more fun.

Camping Overnight with Primo

Does riding Primo bring out the dreamer in you? If so, then camping overnight with Primo and a responsible (probably older) buddy can be a fantasy-come-true. Whether your campsite is just over the ridge from the barn, at a nearby state park or hundreds of miles away from home, there are some things that you should know.

- A Western saddle is ideal for camping because of its comfort and cargo capacity. Even so, pack lightly for yourself (beverage, trail food, a coverup, a change of clothes and a bedroll) and leave room for Primo's things. He will need a halter and a stake-out rope. Ideally, there'll be good grazing wherever you pitch camp. If not, you'll need to bring feed. Carry a first-aid kit and include some gauze wraps in it for Primo. (He can share your other medication for wounds.) Don't forget to pack a knife and flashlight. If you're spending the night in the woods next to a running creek, water's no problem. If you're headed for an ocean beach, you'll need a bucket to carry water from a place that is off-limits to Primo (a public restroom, for example). You can buy a bucket that folds up and takes very little space.
- Beware of hunters in the area. Buckshot fired by bird hunters isn't as dangerous as a deer slug, but you still want to avoid being in the line of fire. *Never* ride in the woods during deer-hunting season. Avoid places where you see cars parked along the road or gates left open, or if you hear gunfire.
- Carry insect repellents for you and for Primo.
- Find out how Primo feels about being staked out *before* you camp any further than over the ridge from home.

- Camping just over the ridge from home is great, provided you have a dependable buddy and follow all other safety precautions. What follows next is intended for you to show your parents, riding club leaders or other responsible adults.

Here are some campsite possibilities:

- County, state or national parks (Never camp without permission. Always check with park rangers. If horses are allowed, camping may require reservations and maybe a fee). *Bring a map.*
- Check with the U.S. Army Corps of Engineers and the state conservation department's division of forestry.
- Find out about privately owned farms, ranches, even a place in the country. Maybe you can camp on private land and ride on neighboring land (private or park). *Bring a map.*
- Check the classifieds in any horse periodical for listings under "travel" or "vacations."

Using Other Riding Facilities

You may want to take Primo to another arena to practice things that you don't have the equipment to practice on at home. Or, you may just want to go to add a little variety to Primo's life. If such a place belongs to a person or a private riding club, your parents may be asked to sign a release. This is to protect the owner from a lawsuit if you or Primo get hurt on the property. You may have to pay a fee, either as a member or a guest rider.

If the place fit your needs, a fee is fair. After all, it costs money to build and keep it in good order. Even if you don't pay anything, you should offer something in return for the hospitality, especially if you use the facilities regularly. You might offer to help paint or clean up around the place. Whether you ride as a guest or pay a fee, show respect. Leave things in as good or better order than you found them. Do things like set up any barrels you knocked down or pick up any empty cans you see lying around.

CHAPTER 8

———— ◆◖●◗◆ ————

Organized Activities

There are lots of ways for you to enjoy Primo. In organized activities, you can enjoy doing things with other riders and horses. I'd like to introduce you to some of these activities briefly. If you would like more information, you can get in touch with organizations I've listed at the end of the book. You will also find books for further reading listed there.

Competitive Trail Riding and Endurance Riding

Competitive trail riding tests a horse's overall fitness over a tough course ranging from twenty-five to one hundred miles. Lots of training and conditioning of both horse and rider take place before the race. Even what the horse and rider wear is carefully planned.

Each horse is checked by a team of veterinarians before starting. They check his vital signs described in Chapter 10, and his general overall condition. Other checks are made along the way and at the finish line. If, during a checkpoint, a horse is considered too tired to continue, or is injured, the team is eliminated from the race. A horse scores points according to the professional opinion of his condition at the start of the ride. These points are added to points given for his condition at the end of the ride.

Endurance rides add points for degree of fitness (as for competitive rides) *with* how long it takes and the team's order of finish for the total score. Part of the score is for condition, part is for time. To be fair, each horse and rider team competes by class. Each class is made up of teams that have about the same amount of experience. Also, there are classes for young riders and for older riders, classes for horses and for ponies.

In a version of trail racing, called "Ride and Tie," two riders share one horse. One rider rides the horse to a point, dismounts and ties him. Then the rider runs to the next point. Meanwhile, the horse rests until the second rider gets there. It will take a while because the second rider got off at the preceding point and ran. When the second rider catches up, he or she gets to "rest" in the saddle. And so it goes.

Rodeos

Rodeos began in the United States in the early 1870s. Several Western towns and ranches each declare that they got rodeos started. Obviously the same idea occurred more than once. Cowboys from one ranch who claimed that they were better at doing their jobs than cowboys who worked on neighboring ranches began the friendly rivalry now called rodeo. Then Wild Bill Hickok and a few other showmen added stagecoach races, "Indian attacks," fancy shooting and other colorful acts, and took their Wild West shows all over the world. A few such shows are still around, but they're far outnumbered by rodeos and other Western competition. Meanwhile, rodeos and Western riding can be found in many countries outside the United States.

Rodeos involve both team and individual work. More than one cowboy is in the arena at any time during a regular rodeo, but each cowboy competes for individual points. When a cowboy is being scored, the other cowboys (clowns included) are there to help. Rodeo events include riding bucking bulls and horses, calf roping and steer wrestling. Prizes range from money, trailer rigs, saddles and other tack to belt buckles and horse blankets. Competitors that have the most points at the end of each rodeo are awarded prizes. Bigger prizes are awarded at the end of each rodeo season.

Ranch rodeos are patterned after the original rodeos. The cowboys compete in teams of four. There are four events:

1. Team roping (head/heel roping)—one cowboy ropes a steer's head, the other cowboy ropes its heels.
2. Wild cow milking pretty much explains itself.
3. Team penning—three specific cattle are separated from a herd and penned.
4. Calf roping and "branding"—the calf gets roped but isn't actually branded with a hot iron. White powder is used instead.

Youth rodeos are limited to riders eighteen years or younger and have basically the same events as regular rodeos. There are more safety rules, however. The prizes are specially suited to this age group. College scholarships are sometimes awarded.

Some rodeo events are just for girls. These events also have points and prizes. They include barrel racing, pole bending and goat roping.

Barrel Racing

Other than at rodeos, barrel racing is open to both boys and girls. For some reason, more girls compete than boys. One notable exception is Shane Hatch, of Farmington, New Mexico. A 4.0 honor student, Shane was the first boy ever to win the Martha Josey World Championship Junior Barrel Race. This competition, which offers over $60,000 in prize money, saddles, clothes and other trophies, is limited to riders under twenty years of age. Thirteen years old at the time (1988), Shane won it by riding the same ten-year-old gelding, Mr. Revolution Bar, that he had grown up with. Their time, 15.873 seconds, was a record. When asked how he did it, Shane said, "I didn't run this one any different than my other races. I always just look ahead for the next barrel."

The object of barrel racing is simple. Horse and rider cross the flag to start the clock. They ride a cloverleaf pattern around three barrels, then race back past the flag to stop the clock. If a barrel is knocked down, the penalty is added time. If a barrel is missed altogether, the rider is eliminated from the race. The fastest time wins.

Most training for barrel racing is done at slower speeds, usually at a jog or even a walk. This is so both horse and rider can learn the proper pattern and techniques. In other words, the fastest horse doesn't necessarily win the race. A horse can be ruined as a good barrel prospect if he's taken around barrels too fast too soon. At least he'll need retraining.

Barrel-racing clubs and youth rodeos have timed speed events. Youth classes (divided by age groups, starting with seven and under) can include three other races: pole bending, stake racing and flag racing.

Barrel Racing
Sunny guides Rooster around one barrel and already has her eye on the next one, so she can line him up properly. They're just loping this pattern, not galloping fast. Most barrel training is done at a jog or even a walk. Adding speed is the easy part. Good technique takes far more work.

For pole bending, six poles are set up in a straight line at regular intervals. Horse and rider pass the flag down to the last pole and come back by riding a zigzag pattern between the poles. They circle the first pole and repeat the pattern to the end pole, circle it, then race back past the flag. Time penalties are added for any poles missed or knocked down. The fastest time wins.

Stake racing involves running a figure eight around two markers. Flag racing requires moving flags from one place to another.

Horse Shows

General Information

There are many kinds of Western horse shows. Those mentioned here offer stock-seat classes for junior riders (also called youth riders).

Primo can compete in an "open show" whatever his ancestry. In order to compete in a "breed show," however, he must be registered with the breed association. Breed registries that emphasize stock-seat riding include the Appaloosa Horse Club, American Paint Horse Association, Palomino Horse Association, International Buckskin Horse Association, Pony of the Americas Club and American Quarter Horse Association (plus Quarter Pony and Half-Quarter).

The AQHA has a special division for riders eighteen years and younger. The American Junior Quarter Horse Association is highly active. Its nearly 14,000 members (as of 1989) come from every state and a few foreign countries. AJQHA offers these stock-seat classes: Reining, Working Cow Horse, Western Riding, Team Penning, Barrel Racing, Pole Bending, Western Pleasure, Trail, Calf Roping, Dally Team Roping (Heading and Heeling), Breakaway Roping, Cutting and Western Horsemanship.

Junior riders just getting started may enter Youth Novice classes. You may compete in novice classes if you've earned less than 10 performance points. (Points are based on how many horses are actually judged, not just entered, for a class. For example, for 3 to 4 horses, the winner gets half a point. For 15 to 19 horses, the winner gets 3 points, second place gets 2 points, third place gets 1 point, fourth place gets half a point. For classes of 45 or more horses, points go all the way through tenth place.)

Once you earn 25 or more novice points (in open and youth divisions combined), you may finish that year as a novice. But, when that year ends, you can no longer compete as a novice. A junior rider may compete both in the youth and the open division.

"Open" means just that: open to all ages and levels of experience. Adults can be either amateur or professional. You may ride as an amateur all your life *unless* you lose your amateur rating. An amateur can win prize money. Prize money is not considered pay. But if you're paid (this includes getting your entry fees and expenses paid as well as collecting a fee), then you must compete as a professional. A professional might be paid for instructing a rider, showing a horse or for judging an event.

Youth are automatically considered amateurs. Youth competition is divided into age categories: 11 and under, 12 to 14 and 15 to 18 years old. A wide variety of awards are offered, from ribbons and trophies to college scholarships.

Each breed registry has its own association. So do various show organizations. They all have rule books that describe the divisions, classes, procedures, what the rider wears, what the horse wears, and so forth.

Western competition is gaining popularity in some breed associations where you'd never expect to find a stock seat. The Tennessee Walking Horse Breeders' and Exhibitors' Association Youth Division (17 years and under) offers six stock-seat classes: Western Pleasure, Competitive or Endurance, Trail, Barrel Racing, Pole Bending and Western Riding. The American Saddlebred International Youth Program has stock-seat classes in its Horsemanship Division.

Show organizations other than breed associations that have events for stock seat include the National Cutting Horse Association, National Reining Horse Association, National

Snaffle Bit Association and American Horse Shows Association. These associations all have Junior Divisions (and rules).

The American Horse Shows Association had a Junior membership total of nearly 10,000 in 1989. The AHSA offers Stock Seat Equitation Medal qualifying classes to junior riders at all recognized shows. To be eligible to compete, the rider must be a junior member of the AHSA. In California and Nevada, the rider must collect 10 points to qualify for the AHSA Stock Seat Medal Finals, and in all other states, one blue ribbon qualifies a rider for the Finals. Finals are held each November at the Grand National Horse Show in San Francisco, California. Excellent prizes and recognition are offered.

Description of Events

Stock Seat Equitation: Riders enter the ring together (as a class) at a walk or jog. They are judged at a walk, jog and lope in both directions in the ring (which requires reversing). Then each rider is asked to perform at least two tests out of eleven that are listed in the AHSA rules. The tests are:

1. Back.
2. Individual performance on the rail.
3. Figure eight at the jog.
4. Lope and stop.
5. Figure eight on correct lead, demonstrating simple change of lead (this is a change whereby the horse is brought back into walk or jog and restarted into a lope on the opposite lead). One figure eight demonstrates two changes of lead and is completed by closing up the last circle and stopping in the center of the eight.
6. Figure eight at lope on correct lead, demonstrating flying change of lead.

7. Change leads down center of ring, demonstrating simple change of lead.
8. Ride serpentine course, demonstrating flying change of lead at each change of direction.
9. Demonstrate sliding stop.
10. Execute 360-degree turns (spins).
11. Rollbacks.

Western Pleasure: This shows the horse to have a pleasant way of doing all three gaits and to change leads, reverse (at the walk or jog only) and back up.

Western Riding: This puts the horse through patterns and routines designed to show that he's sensible, well-mannered, free and easy moving. The horse must position himself for the rider to open and shut a gate. Then he'll walk, jog and lope a particular pattern between markers, step over a log, back up and stop.

Trail Horse: This class is judged on how the horse performs over obstacles, using all three gaits, change of leads, backing and lateral movements. His manners, response to the rider and attitude are very important. With the obstacles listed below, it's understood that the horse and rider work as a team. So I don't say "the horse does" or "the rider does." These four obstacles are often presented:

1. Open, pass through and close a gate.
2. Ride over at least four logs or poles.
3. Back through one of several courses that require turns on the foreleg and the haunches.
4. Side pass a course arranged in one of several patterns.

Two more obstacles are chosen from this group:

1. Cross a water hazard (real or a plastic sheet).
2. Hobble (the horse's front legs are loosely tied together) or ground tie (the horse won't move as long as the reins are dropped to the ground).
3. Carry an object from one part of the arena to the other.
4. Put on and take off a slicker.
5. Remove and replace materials from a mailbox.
6. Cross a bridge.

Reining: Reining competition is based on how well the horse performs a given pattern. The pattern will include circles, runs and sliding stops, changes of lead, backing and spins, with mandatory markers. Several different patterns are described in the rule book. (The American Quarter Horse Association has six, the American Paint Horse has nine.) The judge chooses one, and each contestant follows that pattern.

Cutting: The horse has two and a half minutes to show what he can do to help the rider work the cattle. To do this, he chooses a cow and cuts it (separates it) from the herd. The horse performs some impressive moves to block the cow, who is desperate to rejoin the herd. When his rider gives the signal, the horse backs off and lets the cow go.

Working Cow Horse: This event, which combines reining with cutting, has two parts. It begins with the rider taking his or her horse through a pattern to show that the horse has all the right moves for working cows. The second part adds cattle and puts these moves to the test. The horse gets two and a half minutes for the cattle.

Other stock-seat classes include barrel racing, pole bending, stake racing, and roping events. They are described on pages 172 to 175.

Cutter at Work
Kyle Manion rides his AQHA cutting horse champion, Smooth
Eliminator. (Used with permission of Teresa Jett)

How to Get Started

Although Primo may already have show experience, you
probably haven't. If you plan to show him, you'll both need
to get used to performing in different surroundings. This is
especially true for events held in an indoor arena or at night.
The lights and sounds are different from those of outdoor
and daytime shows. The smells are different, too. Primo will
notice this more than you will. Go to your first show just
to get the feel of the carnival atmosphere. Groom Primo and
warm him up. Don't hang around the in-gate and get in the
way of competitors, however. Walk around, watch other
riders and ask questions. Enter Primo in an easy class or

two. It will give you both confidence and you'll do better when you go to the next show.

It doesn't cost a fortune to campaign Primo to local shows. That's where you both should start, regardless of your ambition.

You might want to get started with Fun Days. Usually sponsored by the 4-H, FFA, Pony Club or a local saddle club, a Fun Day features classes for basic horsemanship, horseback games and novelty contests, such as rider/horse costume classes and musical chairs.

In 1975, the National FFA Organization (formerly Future Farmers of America) introduced a national horse proficiency award to encourage members to explore careers in the horse industry. But crop and livestock matters still rule this organization. The 4-H likewise leans toward agricultural production. However, member interest in horses has created a demand for a more horse-oriented program. With around 200,000 members nationwide, the 4-H horse program provides opportunities for youngsters to learn responsibility and have fun. It teaches through local chapters, using material available from the national 4-H office. The competition advances from a local through a national level.

If you enjoy learning and competing in groups, check on what's available in your area for any of the organizations for young riders described in this chapter or any others you may discover on your own. Start with local competition, then decide whether or not you want to invest in busier, big-league, more expensive competition.

It's not possible to mention every youth organization, but this will set you thinking. For a list of associations for young riders, see pages 206 to 208.

CHAPTER 9

---◆◉◆---

What Is
Primo Thinking?

To think like a horse, you need to know what *he* is thinking. Primo's thoughts are based upon his instincts. His instincts are geared to his survival within the herd.

Pecking Order Within the Herd

Whether he's wild or tame, a horse bases his actions and his attitude on where he fits within the herd. "Pecking order" is the expression used to describe a chain of command that develops within each group of sociable creatures, including chickens, horses and even people. Within each herd, one horse has the first claim on everything. She (usually it's a mare) has her choice of food, water, a place in the shade, and so on. This horse is the alpha (meaning highest) horse of the herd. Not even the herd's stallion will threaten her. Next is the beta (second highest) horse. The alpha is the only horse in the herd who dares to challenge the beta. So it goes, down to the omega horse (last). The poor omega can't out-bluff his own shadow.

The alpha is not always the strongest, fastest or even the

smartest horse in the herd. Usually she's an older mare who's been around for quite a while. It's hard for us to understand how the alpha and beta horses are picked, and how the herd decides who's next. Horses have their own standards.

Things are usually peaceful within the herd. Every horse seems to know his or her place and accept it. This peace doesn't just happen automatically, however. Foals and new horses entering a herd all want to belong, but they must learn how and where to fit in.

A foal learns good herd manners by watching and then copying what he or she sees the other horses do. If Junior forgets or ignores his lessons, he is immediately and clearly disciplined by his mother. Once he learns the rules (which never change) he seldom needs an actual blow. Pinned-back ears and a warning swing of a higher-up horse's hindquarters quickly remind Junior in case he forgets.

Other horses added to the herd have to find out where they fit in the pecking order. They go through a period of trial and error until they find the right spot. This is why you should not ride Primo into the same pasture with a strange herd of horses. The other horses would view Primo as a new member of the herd. His position within that herd's pecking order would be the subject of an immediate "discussion." You do not want to be caught in the middle of an argument between horses!

Anytime a new horse is added to the herd, he should be separated from the rest of the horses by a fence for about a week. This lets them work things out with less chance of fighting. Squealing and near-miss kicking from time to time are normal. It's mostly from excitement, like kids letting off steam on the playground at school.

Once Primo is accepted into a herd, he will find one horse

to be his particular friend. Let's call that horse Buddy. Usually he'll have problems with another horse we'll call Trouble. Primo and Trouble won't actually fight, but they'll very often fuss at each other. Most of the time, this is because Primo and Trouble are competing for the same spot in the herd's pecking order. Seldom is this a contest for who will be alpha. It's usually for beta or somewhere further down the line. Alpha always seems to take over without a fight. She is very self-confident.

If Primo lives in your backyard and is the only horse, his herd is made up of two: you and him. Make sure you are alpha to Primo's beta. Don't let Primo rule your herd.

What About Stallions?

Stallions are male horses that can reproduce. Although a stallion can be a pleasure to own and to ride, some of his instincts can make him too much for a youngster to control. That's why most rule books do not allow youth competitors to show stallions. (For example, both the American Quarter Horse and the American Paint Horse Association rules *forbid* stallions in approved youth classes. The American Horse Shows Association allows them "if division rules for the breed of horse ridden permit juniors to ride stallions.")

Very few herds of riding horses include a stallion. Most riding horses are geldings (ex-stallions) or mares. If there *is* a stallion in Primo's herd, however, just treat him like another horse, not like some monster.

Signs of "Herd Fever"

If Primo has "herd fever," that means he's following his strong natural instinct to be with the herd. The following possible situations show a few ways that herd fever and herd behavior might influence Primo.

- Some horses get very upset when they're alone. A shy horse might refuse to work when he is alone with his rider but will do just fine when in the company of another horse that's being ridden.
- If Primo refuses to *walk* back to the barn after a ride, insist that he do so. Yet it's a strong natural instinct for him to want to hurry back to his "home sweet home."
- Primo ignores your signals as you ride him in the arena. His mind is on Buddy, who whinnies from the fence every time you ride near the pasture. So you give up on lessons and head for the trails (making it *your* idea). Two mornings later, you don't find Primo. He got out of the pasture during the night. Just before you panic, you take another look around and breathe a sigh of relief for the herd instinct. You see Primo. He's outside, but he's standing next to the fence. Rather than wander off to unfamiliar territory alone, he's right across the fence from Buddy.

Overall, herd fever is perfectly normal. The only time it gets to be a problem is when Primo becomes so dependent upon Buddy that you can't do anything with Primo unless Buddy is right there. Usually you can see this situation coming before it gets very bad. If you suspect it's developing, ride Primo somewhere that's out of sight and calling distance of Buddy every chance you get. Be patient yet firm with him. Insist that he walk back home, even if you have to lead him back to the barn.

Primo's Order of Senses

All living creatures use their natural senses for keeping in touch with their surroundings. The five natural senses are seeing, hearing, smelling, tasting and feeling. You learned in Chapter 2 how to use Primo's strong sense of feel and your own sense of feel for communicating most of your natural aids. When you realized that Primo has a "sixth sense" (think-talk), you probably guessed that this is a strong sense, too. A sixth sense is not officially recognized. It's usually thought to be a kind of instinct. We can't rank its importance exactly. Off the record, it may be number one.

In Chapter 1 you learned to approach Primo's shoulder and work your way up to his head. Maybe you figured out why you should do this after reading the trail riding section in Chapter 7, the part about his eyes and the two sides of his brain. If you stood in front of Primo at his blind spot, he could be startled by seeing movement (your hand) headed straight toward his face from nowhere ("nowhere" being anywhere he can't see). Since he also has a blind spot directly behind him, always let him know it's *you* back there before you groom his tail, clean his back feet or cross around him.

You also learned in Chapter 1 not to let Primo exchange greetings with a strange horse. This act involves smelling and tasting. Primo's senses of smell and taste rank next to his sense of feel. His sense of hearing follows. Primo's vision is his least important sense.

How Primo Learns

Primo learns by example. He does what he sees other horses do. Some things that Primo does, however, he does instinctively. He doesn't *learn* such basic things as how to eat, drink, sleep and run from scary things. But he *develops* these instincts. He becomes more skillful by imitating other horses and experimenting.

Most of what Primo learns as a saddle horse, however, is taught by a combination of repetition and reward. A good trainer sets things up so that a green horse is faced with a new situation. Then he encourages the horse to figure out what he's supposed to do. The horse is coaxed, not forced. The moment he makes a correct response (maybe not perfect, but definitely an effort in the right direction), he's rewarded. Again and again he's asked to do something, and he's rewarded for any progress.

Now that you're riding Primo, he continues to do what has become a familiar routine. He may or may not *enjoy* the routine, but he's learned what to expect. He feels safe while doing these things. You can see how important it is for you (as his new trainer, so to speak) to be patient and take each step slowly. Primo (and you) will learn some things faster than others, but it never pays in the long run to rush any stage of a horse's (or rider's) training.

A few lessons, however, are learned immediately. They find a direct path to the brain, usually by way of surprise. Unfortunately, these usually are the few things we do *not* want Primo to remember. If, for example, Primo has a bad hauling experience, you may need special help to get him loaded until he's finally learned to trust trailers again.

How Primo Communicates

Primo uses different parts of his body to express specific things. By learning his body language, you can understand what he's thinking. A great way to learn is by watching him from the sidelines when he's out in the pasture with other horses. Watch him also at mealtimes—before, during and after he eats. Watch his responses to being groomed and tacked up. Notice how he responds to anything added to his barn and pasture. Watch him when the weather changes. Study him every chance you get. You can usually figure out what Primo means by watching long enough to see what's going on. Match what you see happening to Primo with what you know about your own natural routines and feelings, such as hunger, fear, pain, loneliness, joy, jealousy, the urge to protect and so forth. Some people never realize that horses actually have all these feelings, too. In fact, horses are very emotional creatures.

You can tell someone's mood just by watching that person, can't you? The same is true for a horse. Many of the gestures that Primo uses to express himself are the same gestures people use. His overall appearance is relaxed when he's contented and he becomes tense when he is upset or excited. Primo's feelings are expressed most clearly by his ears, eyes, muzzle and tail. Next come his neck and legs.

When Primo's ears are loosely angled to the side, he is relaxed. When they're pointed forward or back, he's concentrating on something in front of or behind him. If they're flattened back, he's angry (or pretending to be).

Primo's eyes show how he feels, much the way your eyes show how you feel. If he's concentrating on his own feelings (maybe he's in pain or angry), he'll squint. Fear makes his eyes open wide and show the whites (sclera). Contentment makes them droopy.

His muzzle takes the place of your mouth, nose and chin for expressing feelings. When you are relaxed, however, your lower lip doesn't droop quite as much as Primo's lower lip! Primo purses his lip and wrinkles his chin and nose for the same reasons you do. For example, when Primo picks up a really strange or fascinating scent, his way of showing it is to raise his nose and curl up his upper lip in what is called the flehmen posture. He looks like he's laughing.

Primo's tail is raised proudly to express joy and show authority. It's tucked tightly to show fear or insecurity. It's held anywhere in between, according to how alert he is (up for more, down for less). He switches his tail to show his irritation, and, of course, to chase off bugs.

Primo uses his neck to snake out his head as a show of authority. He arches it to show excitement and lowers it when he's relaxed. He moves his neck in response to what you ask with your aids. He also uses it to position his head so that he can see, hear or smell something better.

Primo uses his legs and feet to move around for any reason, including "fight or flight" situations. He uses his feet to dig for food. The food can be real, as in grass buried under snow, or imaginary. For instance, sometimes he'll paw impatiently for his dinner or even while eating it. His feet and legs often express warnings. A turned hip or a cocked hind foot warn "Look out or I'll kick." Trembling movements of the legs or upper quarters (front or back) show a building excitement or fear.

Communicating with Primo

Communication isn't just a matter of your telling Primo what to do. It's an *exchange* of messages between you and Primo. Here are some guidelines to help you understand the logic behind his signals.

For example, you understand that Primo's eyesight is the physical cause for his sudden fear of harmless moving objects ("horse eaters"), but you can't let him get away with misbehaving and you don't want to be unfair. What can you do?

Be patient yet firm. Gently insist that he face the monster. Praise him for any sign of progress and go on to something else. Then (same day or later, depending on what the feared object is), come back. Wear a hard hat if there's any danger of your being thrown. (Better yet, wear a safety helmet whenever you ride.) However, do not assume that Primo will continue to put up a fight. That's using think-talk to your disadvantage, not as a help. Picture Primo accepting or downright ignoring the problem. Keep showing him the same monster until he finally understands that it won't hurt him, and he accepts it with no fear at all.

Anytime you approach a strange horse, respect his private space. Don't cross the invisible boundary line until he's had time to get used to you. Generally, this doesn't take more than a moment or two, but it's a necessary step. Skipping it feels to him like you'd feel if a perfect stranger walked into your house without first knocking on the door and asking to come in. Crossing the outer limit puts the animal on guard. Crossing the next line makes him retreat and take flight. Crossing the innermost line forces the animal to attack and fight. If you concentrate on his body language, and follow your own instincts, he'll tell you where those lines are.

Once a horse knows you, you're usually admitted to his innermost space. Sometimes, as with a terrified horse or a nervous mare and her newborn foal, you have to move away and start all over again. Don't run off. Just wait.

Primo reads your body language very well. He understands your firm, springy stride of self-confidence. He knows the difference between that kind of approach and the way you look when you try to sneak up on him because you're afraid he'll run off.

If you have trouble approaching Primo to halter him, you'll be less of a threat if you bow your head and drop your leading shoulder slightly, and move along smoothly.

A raised chin and leading shoulder, on the other hand, represent authority. Add an outstretched hand and you can stop Primo just like a policeman stops oncoming traffic. In either case, think-talk is a powerful tool. Mentally picture what you want to happen, *not what you're afraid might happen*.

To Primo, how you hold yourself shows how you feel. You unconsciously hold yourself differently when you're sad or worried than when you're happy or proud. Primo is very aware of these differences in your body language.

You see Primo and the rest of the herd communicate with their bodies. Once you have Primo's attention, you can use your body to communicate commands. With practice, you can even control him (especially in a pen) without a rope:

- Tuck your shoulder (or hip) in and lean the other way to pull Primo toward you.
- Thrust yourself out toward him to push him away from you.
- Step with authority toward his rump to push him forward.
- Do the same toward his shoulder to turn or stop him. Whether he turns or stops depends on how much force you use and whether there's a fence to help you.

If Primo would rather play tag in the pasture than let you catch him, there are two ways to deal with this.

One is not to chase him. Instead, squat down and appear fascinated with something on the ground (supposedly ignoring Primo). After a moment or so, his curiosity outweighs his urge to stay out of your reach. He approaches and peers over your shoulder to see what's there (and if it's good to eat). The game is over. All you need to do is calmly speak to him, hug him and, while you're conveniently close, slip on the halter.

For the second way, you may have to be more aggressive to catch him. Thrust out your shoulder nearest him. "Snake" your head at him and maybe stomp your foot, but keep your arms down. When Primo halts and looks at you in amazement, drop your gaze and move toward him until you are close enough to reach out (to the shoulder/neck, remember?) and smoothly grab him in a hug-hold. Then halter him.

If he starts to leave, walk after him. *Never* run or even get in a hurry. Match his moves. Every time *he* turns, *you* turn to head him off or at least keep even with him. It's likely that he'll keep more or less in a circle around you, even in a big pasture. Primo's not really afraid of you. He knows you won't hurt him. He just needs to be convinced of who's boss, who's alpha.

Sooner or later, he'll come to a full stop. He'll sigh as a sign of accepting his fate. Take advantage of this moment and move smoothly toward him without delay. If you miss it, you'll have to start all over. Don't rush, but don't be timid either. Just move with quiet authority to claim your prize.

It'll require some acting and experimenting on your part, at first, to use body-talk along with think-talk on Primo. Once you begin to succeed, however, you can build on. You can develop a large vocabulary of body-talk. Just believe in yourself and "listen" to Primo.

CHAPTER 10

———◆◄●►◆———

An Ounce
of Prevention

There's an old saying, "An ounce of prevention is worth a pound of cure." It's better to take a few steps to protect Primo and yourself when everything is going well than to skip those steps and end up with a big problem that could have been prevented. Even though this is not a book about how to take care of Primo, you have been learning about basic care all along. You know, for instance, to take care of your tack, check Primo's feet before each ride, start each ride out slowly and finish it at a walk (so that Primo can warm up and cool down) and use the buddy system, among other things. These are "ounces of prevention."

Primo's Vital Signs and How to Find Them

Every living creature has four vital signs that show whether it is healthy or not. The signs are temperature, pulse rate, respiration and capillary refill time. Good health is based upon what is normal for each sign. For example, normally your body heat measures 98.6 degrees on a Fahrenheit thermometer. If it's one degree above or below that, you might be sick. Sometimes your temperature could be one or two degrees higher because you've been exercising and your body has heated up. As soon as you've had a chance to cool down, your temperature will return to normal. To do this, first you'll breathe faster, then you'll start to sweat. These two are automatic. Third, you need to rest. Fourth, you need to drink extra fluids to replace what was lost by sweating.

It's the same with Primo. He also needs the same four steps to recover after exercise. You can judge his condition by his sweat. Sweat that's clear and watery means that he's in good shape. Sweat that's thick and soapy means that he's not fit. If Primo is out of shape, you'll need to exercise him a little more each time you ride him. Make it a gradual but regular thing. Do *not* try to turn Primo into a super athlete overnight. The reason you start out and finish slow when exercising is to give Primo's body (and your body) an opportunity to make some necessary changes.

A horse's normal temperature (at rest) is between 99 and 101 degrees F. It's usually higher immediately after exercise, but otherwise anything higher than 101.5F is a pretty good indication of infection. A horse's temperature is taken with a veterinary thermometer. Ask your vet or an experienced person to show you how it's done.

Primo's normal pulse rate (at rest) can be between 28 and 50 beats per minute (BPM). It's important that you find out what is normal for Primo. "Normal" can change. The better condition he's in, the lower his resting pulse rate will be. Also, the better condition he's in, the sooner his pulse will drop down to normal after exercise. His pulse rate will be much higher right after exercise. It could be 100 BPM or more. What's important is that it returns to normal (or close to normal, say, under 70) within about ten minutes after exercise. You can feel Primo's pulse in several places:

- On the bony edge under his lower jaw
- Midway between his ear and his eye
- On his foreleg in the fetlock area
- On the outside of his hind leg below the hock
- On his body behind his left elbow.

Because of the pulse's speed, and Primo's jerking movements, it's easier to count his pulse for 15 seconds and multiply the number by 4. (Example: 11 beats in 15 seconds times 4 equals a pulse rate of 44 beats per minute.) Or, count it for 30 seconds and double the number.

Use your fingers (not your thumb) to feel Primo's pulse. Place two or three fingertips on the pulse area and gently push around until you can locate the beat. Hold your fingers steady against that spot while you count.

Primo's normal respiration is between 8 and 16 breaths per minute. You'll see his ribs and flanks move as he breathes. You can count for 15 seconds and multiply by 4, but it's better to watch closely for 30 seconds and then double your count. You'll have plenty of time to count.

Primo's capillary refill time shows how long it takes for his blood to rush back into a place after it has been pressed hard. It usually takes three seconds or less. Two and a half seconds is ideal. Too fast usually indicates infection, and too slow can mean the horse is in shock. Fold back Primo's upper lip and look at his gums. (They should be pink. If they're blue, gray, red or purple, call the vet.) Press your finger (not the nail) into his gum. When you remove it, there'll be a white spot where your finger was. Time how long it takes for the gum to turn pink again. Watch and count: "Thousand one . . . thousand two . . ." and so on.

If Primo becomes dehydrated, he could be in serious trouble. The usual cause is getting overheated. Use the "pinched

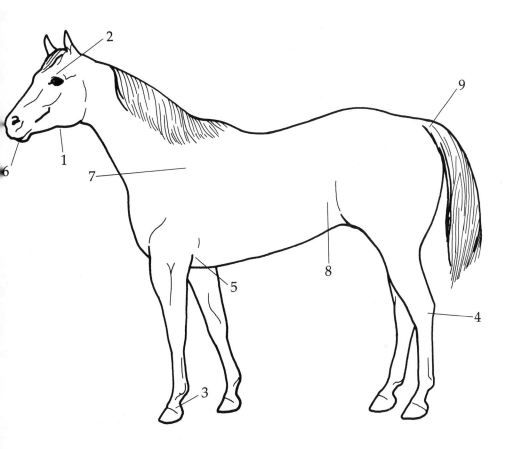

Checking Primo's Vital Signs

Primo's pulse can be located: (1) at the bony edge along his jaw, (2) midway between his ear and eye, (3) on the outside fetlock area of his foreleg, (4) just below his hock on the outer side and (5) at his girth behind his left elbow. Normal, at rest, is anywhere between 28 and 50 beats per minute. Check his capillary refill time at his gums (6). Normal is about two seconds. Give him the pinch test for dehydration at his shoulder or neck (7). Normally, rested or not, the fold will flatten out promptly when released. Watch his flanks (8) move to count his breaths. Normally, at rest, Primo breathes between 8 and 16 times per minute. Use a rectal (9) equine thermometer with a safety clip to take his temperature. Normal, at rest, is 99 to 101 degrees.

skin" test to check him for dehydration. Pinch a fold of skin on his shoulder or just above his eye and then release the fold. If it returns promptly, Primo's body fluid level is okay. But if the pinch holds its shape for two seconds or more, he needs fluid replacement and a vet's immediate attention. Plain drinking water will help but won't solve the problem entirely. A dehydrated horse needs electrolytes (certain vital chemicals that stay in body fluids) replaced.

Other Concerns

It's common sense not to ride Primo when he's injured without checking to see whether the injury is serious. Major cuts need attention from the vet, but you can take care of simple cuts yourself and keep them clean. Spray on or apply repellent to keep insects off his wounds. (Don't spray directly into a wound.) If Primo limps, clean his feet extra carefully (he might have a stone lodged in his foot) and check for puncture wounds. Feel his entire foot for hot spots. Lameness, not wanting to move and clearly appearing uncomfortable are matters that should not be ignored. If Primo still limps after you've cleaned his feet, ask for help. While grooming Primo before a ride, make it a habit to check for cuts and swellings. Check him again after you remove his tack.

Being sick is not as obvious as being injured. If Primo looks under the weather, check his vital signs. Any time they're not normal, don't ride him. In fact, you probably should call a vet. Before you make the call, however, have Primo's vital signs ready so that you can tell the vet over the phone. Besides Primo's vital signs, remember what you learned in Chapter 9 about Primo's body language. Use that as well as other clues, such as a lack of appetite or any changes in his urine or manure.

Guidelines for Protecting Primo

Here are some guidelines for keeping Primo safe and healthy, so that he'll always be ready for you to ride.

Primo must be fed and watered regularly. He should be fed at the same times, generally early morning and late afternoon, not just whenever you get around to it. Feed him after you ride, not before, and give him time to cool down before he eats. Changes in how much Primo's fed, or any other changes in his diet, should be made gradually, not all at once. He *must* have access to fresh water at all times, and he needs a salt block.

Primo needs three things done on a regular basis:

- He needs a farrier to trim his feet and/or shoe him every four to six weeks.
- He needs a vet to check his teeth and inoculate him (usually twice a year, depending on where you live).
- He *must* be wormed every four to eight weeks, depending on which worming product your vet recommends that you use.

Worming is important. Otherwise, Primo won't get the full benefit of his food. Worse still, he can get colic faster from having a belly full of worms than from any other cause. Colic is the number one killer of horses.

Other "must have's" for Primo are protection from bugs, a safe shelter, and companionship (even if you're his only herd buddy).

Safe shelter includes his pasture. Patrol Primo's pasture

on a regular basis for poisonous plants, bad fencing or gates and other objects that can injure him, such as glass and pieces of board with nails sticking up.

Horses, cows and other animals that graze can die from eating toxic (poisonous) plants. Your local County Extension Agent can tell you what dangerous plants grow in your area and show you what they look like. Fortunately *most* poisonous plants don't taste as good to Primo as grass. They're only eaten when the grazing is poor. It's natural for horses to want to graze off and on all day and at night, too, if they're turned out. Having good hay to eat can reduce the risk of Primo's eating toxic plants when there's no more grass or other plants that are safe for him to eat.

Remember: The special union between you and Primo requires your hard work, patience, determination, kindness, tact and, of course, experience. But if you truly care for your horse and work to develop an understanding with him, you will not only have a friend, you will gain greater courage, confidence and awareness of yourself.

APPENDIX 1

———— ◆•◆•◆ ————

Books to Read for More Information

General Information

Horse Industry Directory is published by the American Horse Council, 1700 K Street, N.W., Washington, D.C. 20006, (202) 296-4031. A new directory comes out each year, with addresses updated for all organizations, registries, government sources, horse magazines and other trade publications plus equine health and educational data. Price is $10.00.

The American Horse Council also publishes a "Basic Horse Safety Manual" for $2.00. Geared to youth, this 19-page illustrated booklet has advice on fire safety and prevention, trail riding, headgear, tack and more.

The following books should be available at your local bookstore, or ask at your library.

Tack

The Howell Book of Saddlery and Tack by Elwyn Harley-Edwards (Howell Book House, $24.95)

> Filled with photos and illustrations, this is a colorful guide about equipment from around the world. It's a resource on topics ranging from the history of saddles to the use of training aids.

Tack Buyer's Guide by Charlene Strickland (Breakthrough Publications, $24.95)

> This is a complete handbook on the purchase and use of all kinds of tack: saddles, bridles, bits, blankets, barn equipment, specialty gear and much more. It tells how to recognize the good brands and gives money-saving tips that work.

Horse Care

Horse Owner's Veterinary Handbook by James M. Griffin, M.D. and Tom Gore, D.V.M. (Howell Book House, $24.95)

Presents vital information in an easy-to-understand format, with a detailed table of contents. Special feature: index of signs (for example: "muscle spasm," "peculiar stance") helps to determine what sorts of problems a horse may have.

Western Horsemanship

The Art of Western Riding by Bob Mayhew with John Birdsall (Howell Book House, $22.50)

Bob Mayhew, who lives in England, wrote this initially to teach Western riding to Europeans. It's equally good for beginners and for experienced English riders who want to change styles.

Think Harmony With Horses by Ray Hunt (Pioneer Publishing Co., $12.95)

Ray Hunt travels all over the country, teaching riders how to unite both mind and body with horses. He revolutionized the Western way of schooling a horse by thinking harmony, as opposed to the rough old method of breaking a horse.

Western Training: Theory and Practice by Jack Brainard with Peter Phinny (The Western Horseman, Inc., $12.95)

This is a common-sense guide to Western training written by a horseman who lives right up the road from me. It stresses the need to look at training from the horse's viewpoint, to try and analyze what the horse is trying to tell the rider/ trainer, and to realize the importance of patience for producing the most lasting results.

If you can't find the books listed here at your local bookstore or library, try a Direct Book Marketer who specializes in horse books. They produce original new books and reprints of horse books (including some classics) that are no longer available at the original publishing horse or at regular book-

stores. Horse catalogs, where you can also order tack for
Primo, are good sources. (Prices may vary, by the way.)
Here are some direct marketers who offer free catalogs:

- Breakthrough Publications, Inc., Millwood, NY 10546, (800)
  824-5000.
- H. Kaufmann & Sons, 419 Park Avenue South, New York,
  NY 10016.
- Miller's, 123 East 24th St., New York, NY 10010.
- The Practice Ring, Inc., 7510 Allisonville Rd., Indianapolis,
  IN 64250, (800) 553-5219.
- Schneiders Saddlery, 1609 Golden Gate Plaza, Cleveland,
  OH 44124 and 6245 East Bell Rd., Scottsdale, AZ 85254,
  (800) 365-1311 for a full-line horse catalog.

APPENDIX 2

———◆◄◉►◆———

AHSA Equitation Seat Chart*

	Good	Minor Faults	Major Faults	Elimination
SEAT	keeping center of balance complete contact with saddle straight back	sitting off center sway back round back losing center of balance	excessive body motion popping out of saddle	falling off horse (refer to Art. 3713)

	Good	Minor Faults	Major Faults	Elimination
HANDS	quiet light hands maintaining consistent head position proper position (diagrams on pages 202 and 203 in the *AHSA Rule Book*)	unsteadiness incorrect position	horse's mouth gapping heavy hands constant bumping restrictions causing untrue gaits touching horse less than 16" of rein slack between hands touching saddle to prevent fall	two handing reins finger between romal reins more than one finger between split reins

	Good	Minor Faults	Major Faults	Elimination
LEGS	secure leg position proper weight in stirrups controlling motion weight evenly on ball of foot	uneven stirrups motion in legs insufficient weight in	excess spurring loss of contact between legs &	touching in front of cinch

	Good	*Minor Faults*	*Major Faults*	*Elimination*
	heels lower than toes	stirrups incorrect position	saddle/ foot & stirrups loss of stirrup	

	Good	*Minor Faults*	*Major Faults*	*Elimination*
CONTROL	maintaining horse in good form at consistent gaits ability to maintain horse under adverse conditions	breaking from walk to jog breaking from jog to lope not standing in line up	breaking from jog to walk breaking from lope to jog allowing horse to back crooked missing leads failure to back	[none]

	Good	*Minor Faults*	*Major Faults*	*Elimination*
OVERALL APPEARANCE	suitable well-fitted outfit well-groomed horse clean equipment	saddle not suitable to rider's size unfitted outfit dirty boots ungroomed horse uncleaned equipment	improper appointments	illegal equipment

	Good	*Minor Faults*	*Major Faults*	*Elimination*
GENERAL	good attitude towards horse and judge consistency of rider's form	equipment not fitting horse failure to use corners and rail suitability of horse and rider	excessive voice commands excessive circling major delays in transitions	schooling horse off pattern

APPENDIX 3

————◆◆▶▸————

Associations for Young Riders

It is not possible to give the name and address of every association involved with youth stock-seat riding. What follows is a sampling to get you started. If Primo is breed-registered, contact the national registry for a local club. If you need more help finding an address, try the American Horse Council, 1700 K Street NW, Suite 300, Washington, D.C. 20006 (phone 202/296-4031).

• American Endurance Ride Conference does not have a separate youth division, but it does award the highest scoring youth in a competition. Ride and Tie Association recognizes the youngest winning team. Contact AERC at 701 High Street #203, Auburn, CA 95603 (phone 916/823-2260); or Ride and Tie, 1865 Indian Valley Road, Novato, CA 94947 (phone 415/897-1829).

• American Horse Shows Association has a stock seat medal class for Junior members (under 18) of the AHSA. Contact AHSA Stock Seat Equitation Committee, 220 East 42nd Street, New York, NY 10017-5806 (phone 212/972-2472).

• American Junior Rodeo Association, Box 481, Rankin, TX 79778 (no phone) oversees many rodeo events for youth.

• American Morgan Horse Association Youth is one of several breed associations offering youth divisions that are aimed more for 4-H and FFA horse-awareness programs than for show competition. For information contact AMHA Inc., P.O. Box 960, Shelburne, VT 05482 (phone 802/985-4844).

• American Paint Horse Association has a program for Junior (18-under) competition (AJPHA). They also have an Outside Competitive Activities program that gives credit and recognition for members who participate in approved shows and activities outside of APHA. Contact AJPHA at P.O. Box 961023, Fort Worth, TX 76161 (phone 817/439-3400).

• American Quarter Horse Association has an outside activities program, too, plus two programs for young members. Their Junior division (AJQHA) focuses on young riders interested in competition. The other program has a reward-type plan for riding a Quarter Horse. After riding fifty hours, for example, you get a patch. Contact AJQHA or the AQHA Horseback Riding Program at P.O. Box 200, Amarillo, TX 79168 (phone 806/376-4811).

• Appaloosa Horse Club has a good youth program and network of regional clubs. Contact ApHC, Inc., P.O. Box 8403, Moscow, ID 83483 (phone 208/882-5578).

• Future Farmers of America is an educational group that recently added a horse program. Ask your school office for information about local chapters. Or, contact National FFA Organizations, P.O. Box 15160, Alexandria, VA 22309 (phone 703/ 360-3600).

• International Arabian Horse Association includes Arabians, Half-Arabians and Anglo-Arabians. For information on youth stock-seat activities, contact IAHA at P.O. Box 3396, Denver, CO 80233 (phone 303/450-4774).

• Josey Enterprises, Inc. (Route 2 Box 235, Karnack, TX 75661, phone 903/935-5358) has complete information on barrel racing and calf roping, including a list of clubs.

• National Cutting Horse Association is one example of a breed-approved "outside activity." For information on their Youth Division (18 and under), contact NCHA, 4704 Highway 377 South, Fort Worth, TX 76116–8805 (phone 817/244-6188).

• National 4-H Council is a youth program for riders 9 to 19. Look under Cooperative Extension Service in your local telephone directory under county or governmental agency listings. Ask if they have a local 4-H horse program or club. If not, contact National 4-H Supply Service, 7100 Connecticut Avenue, Chevy Chase, MD 20815 (phone 301/961-2945).

• National Reining Horse Association is another example of breed-approved "outside activity." For information about their Youth Division, contact NRHA, 28881 SR 83, Coshocton, OH 43812 (phone 614/622-5611).

• National Little Britches Rodeo is for riders 8 to 18. For information, contact NLBR, 1045 West Rio Grande, Colorado Springs, CO 80906 (phone 719/389-0333).

• National High School Rodeo Association is for riders in grades 9 to 12. Contact NHSRA, 12200 Pecos, #120, Denver, CO 80234 (phone 303/452-0820).

INDEX

————————

SHELBY